DEDICATION

I would like to dedicate this book to my high school sweetheart and wonderful wife, Donna. You have continued to support me and my crazy, insane ideas for over 44 years, and for that I will be eternally grateful. You are the best!

ACKNOWLEDGMENTS

First and most important, I would like to thank the students I have had over the many years I have been teaching. You continually inspire me with your accomplishments and creativity.

I also want to thank Susanne Woods for encouraging me to submit the proposal for this book.

To Liz Aneloski, my editor extraordinaire, a special thank-you for taking a machine quilter and making him look like an author (no easy task).

INTRODUCTION

Hello, machine quilters and would-be machine quilters. I would like to say a few words about the idea behind and the reason for this book.

In the time since I began machine quilting, I have seen a radical evolution in the quilting world. Machine quilting has gone from a dirty word to an accepted art form.

There are a lot of true artists doing amazing commercial machine quilting. The downside to having one of these artists do your quilting for you is that the cost is going to be much, much higher than if you do it yourself. Good work takes time, and time is money for those in the business.

The other downside is that you also run the risk of not getting the design or quality that you expected when you turned your pride and joy over to someone else. Along with the quality machine-quilting artists, as in any industry, there are also those who produce substandard results. You would not believe the horror stories I have heard from unhappy customers who have had their quilts ruined by someone else, and they still had to pay for shoddy work.

I have long felt that for a piece of work to be truly the owner's, he or she should create it from start to finish. That way, the piece is unique to the person who created it.

It is my goal with this book to present in text and pictures the machine-quilting class I have taught to hundreds of people for over ten years. Rather than just present the techniques, which many others before me have done, I want to address the problems students continually have when learning to machine quilt and provide solutions to those problems.

In addition, it is my feeling that if quilters begin to complete more of their own machine-quilted projects, they will have more money to make more quilts.

I hope this book inspires you and helps you develop the necessary skills to create the next blue-ribbon winner at your local and then national quilt show. The only thing holding you back is you.

CHAPTER 1

Tools, Supplies, and Workspace

The following is a list of some of my favorite products that have worked well for me over the years. Do not be afraid to try other products and to begin your own list of favorite products.

- Hobbs Heirloom Cotton 80/20 batting
- Superior Threads
- Mettler Thread
- Aurifil Thread
- Collins Washable Wonder Marker #C48
- Collins Vanishing Fabric Marker #C28
- General's Chalk Pencils #4473
- Machingers gloves
- SewEzi extension table
- Bendable Bright Light

Necessary Tools and Accessories

Just about any sewing machine can be used to machine quilt if it is set up correctly and operates properly. You certainly do not need the latest, greatest machine that comes out. There are features that may make the process easier, but that doesn't mean that they are essential.

THE MACHINE

The foot control should be able to smoothly control the machine speed from very slow to fast. Some of the very inexpensive machines cannot be operated at a slow speed. They tend to groan and then take off all of a sudden as you press harder on the pedal. This will lead to lots of frustration for quilters of any skill level. If your machine does this, I recommend that you get another machine for machine quilting. It doesn't have to be a new models; there are plenty of perfectly good used ones out there that have been traded in for the latest, greatest one.

Throat opening size (the distance from the needle to the inside of the machine) is a matter of convenience. The larger the opening, the easier it will be to maneuver the quilt sandwich through the machine.

Throat opening comparison

When I started machine quilting, all heirloom machine quilting was done on standard domestic home machines. I have even taught people to machine quilt on Singer Featherweight machines. This doesn't mean it is easy, but it can be done.

I have used one of the longer-arm domestic machines for many years with excellent results. This portable machine is at least ten years old and is used constantly by me and as a loaner to students in my classes. It is not fancy, but it works flawlessly.

My favorite setup is one of the mid-arm machines that has been configured as a sit-down machine.

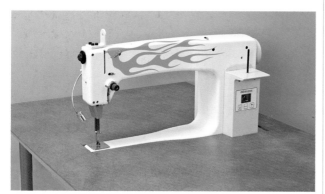

Mid-arm machine as a sit-down quilting machine

Cleaning and Oiling

Your sewing machine should be in good working order and clean. The operation of your machine and the quality of your stitches depend on it. Each time you get ready to do any stitching, it is a good idea to clean out any lint that may have accumulated from your last session. Refer to your owner's manual for guidance.

While you have the machine opened up for cleaning, it is a good time to oil the hook assembly if the manual calls for it. Some of the newer machines do not require any oiling in this area. It seems from my experience that machines with a standard bobbin case will require a drop of oil on the hook, and machines with a rotary hook (drop-in bobbin) will not need oil.

HOPPING/DARNING FOOT

You will also need a spring-loaded foot. This type of foot is commonly called a hopping, darning, or quilting foot. These feet come in a variety of shapes and sizes. Most machines come with one, but there are also many generic feet available.

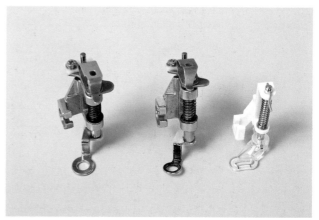

Hopping/darning/quilting feet

My personal favorite is a small oval plastic foot that hops up and down on the quilt sandwich. I take a small X-Acto saw and cut out the front of the foot so my vision is not obstructed by trying to look through the foot. Trying to look through the clear plastic causes distortion, so your stitches will not be where you think they are.

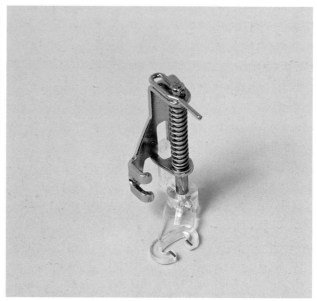

Cut out front of foot.

MACHINE NEEDLES

Most beginners will start using the good old universal needle that came with their machine. A universal needle is designed to do everything, but nothing really well.

I think you will have the best luck if you use a top-stitch needle for your machine-quilting work. This needle is quite sharp and has an elongated eye, which works better when using those fancy decorative threads that are on the market now. It also has a larger groove running down the length of the needle, which helps the thread flow through the quilt better. Superior Threads makes a top-stitch needle especially for machine quilting that is outstanding. It is titanium coated to extend the life of the needle.

Needle size can affect your stitch quality. When you machine piece, there is never any lateral pressure put on the needle, because the machine is only moving forward and occasionally backward. When you free-motion machine quilt, you put pressure on the needle in the direction you are moving your work. As you move the fabric, you cause the needle to flex. If it flexes enough, it will hit the needle plate and snap off. Also, as the needle flexes sideways, it is moved away from the hook that is making the stitch, and the stitch quality is often adversely affected. To compensate for this, I tend to use a larger needle when I machine quilt. My preference is a 90/14 or 100/16, depending on the size of thread I am using. I use the larger needle for thicker thread. The higher the number, the larger the needle size.

NONSLIP PRODUCTS

To machine quilt, you will really need something that will give you a good grip on the quilt sandwich while at the same time allowing you to feel what you are doing. This is important because if your hands are constantly slipping, you will have erratic and inaccurate stitching.

Machingers gloves are my personal favorite. They are made from a lightweight stretch nylon with polyurethane coating on the fingertips, and they come in four sizes, so finding a comfortable fit should not be a problem. The gloves should be snug, but not uncomfortably tight.

For those of you who cannot stand to wear gloves because they are constraining or hot, some quilters use Quick Sort, which is the tacky stuff that bank tellers use when they count money. Before I discovered Machingers, I used the stretchy tape that veterinarians use on animals. A couple of wraps around your fingertips, and you are good to go. If you have a latex allergy, stay away from this tape. You might also want to check out glycerin and Neutrogena Body Emulsion. Both of these products will make your fingers a little tacky, but they should not transfer to your quilt top. If they do, they should easily wash out.

There are other gloves and products on the market, so experiment until you find the product that is just right for you.

Gloves and other grip products

SCISSORS

You will need a small pair of sharp scissors for clipping threads. They should be small, to get in close to your work, and sharp, to easily cut the thread. I like to use small curved embroidery scissors. As a safety measure, I have ground off the sharp points, so I do not have to worry about poking a hole in the quilt.

Scissors with tips rounded

Close-up of rounded tips

SEAM RIPPER

The purpose of this tool is pretty self-explanatory. Sooner or later, we are all going to have stitches that will need to be ripped out and repaired. I suggest that you get a good seam ripper with a thin point that is sharp and finished well. Alex Anderson's 4-in-1 Essential Sewing Tool (C&T Publishing) has a dandy seam ripper built right into it. A nice seam ripper will cost you a little extra money but will be well worth it in the long run. This will be especially true if you have to rip any very small stitches.

In my opinion these are the only things that you absolutely need to machine quilt. The items listed under Optional Accessories (at right) will make machine quilting easier and will help to improve the quality of your stitching but are not absolutely necessary.

Optional Accessories

EXTENSION TABLE

Your home machine, as it comes out of the box or case, just doesn't have a large enough work surface to allow you to machine quilt easily. Some machines come with small extension tables, but in my opinion, even they are not large enough. The problem is twofold. First, the more your quilt drapes unsupported over the edge of your work surface, the harder it will be to move your quilt when you are stitching. Second, you will be fighting to keep your left hand from falling off the machine without a table extension. This will severely limit your range of motion when machine quilting. If you are going to consider some form of extension, get one that is made to fit your machine.

I have recently started using a SewEzi table with my domestic machine, and I just love it.

The table is just the right height for machine quilting, and piecing for that matter. Custom inserts are supplied with the table to fit your machine, so you have a nice flat surface to work on. Last but not least, the table is very portable because it has wheels built right in. It is one of those "why didn't I think of that?" things.

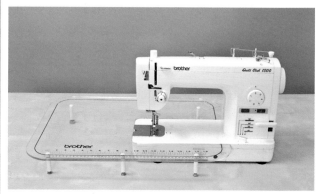

Extension table

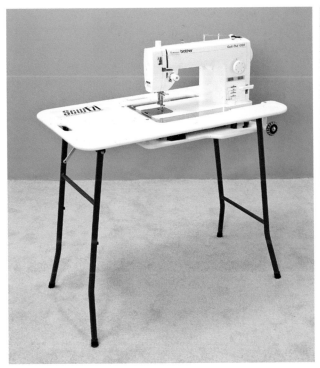

SewEzi table

ADJUSTABLE CHAIR

I recommend that you get an adjustable task chair for your machine quilting, and, in fact, for all of your sewing. Let's face it—the machine sitting at your dining room table is just too darn high. Think back to your mother's or grandmother's old console machine. Now those were the days. When the machine was put away, the top of the cabinet was about the height of your dining room table, and when it was open and ready for sewing, it was still the height of the dining room table. In our modern era, we set the machine on top of the dining room table and wa-lá, the machine is now about 3″ too high to work at comfortably. This is especially true for machine quilting. If you sit at the table in a standard chair, you are going to be reaching up to quilt. This will put a lot of strain on your arms, neck, and shoulders. This in turn will cause you to get tired very quickly.

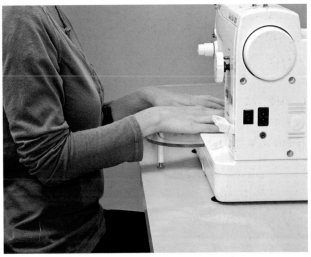

Poor seating posture

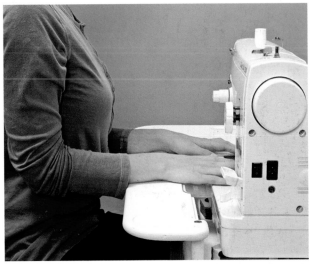

Good seating posture

This is especially true if you happen to be shorter than the center on a basketball team.

A good adjustable chair will allow you to raise yourself up to a reasonable height that will not create undue strain on your arms, neck, and shoulders. You might also want to look at one with lumbar support.

If you find that once you get your chair to the right height, you can't reach the pedal, just put a book or block under the pedal.

EXTRA LIGHTING

The lighting on most machines is totally inadequate for machine quilting. There just isn't enough bright light directed at the needle and surrounding area. I strongly recommend some form of auxiliary lighting. My personal favorite right now is the Bendable Bright Light made by Dream World Inc. This is an LED light that can be directed right where it is needed. It is quite bright and puts out very little heat, which is a great advantage. Small halogen lights are inexpensive and put out quite a lot of light, but they also put out quite a bit of heat.

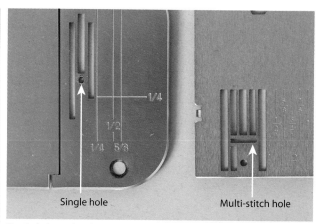

Single hole   Multi-stitch hole

Single hole and multi-stitch needle plates

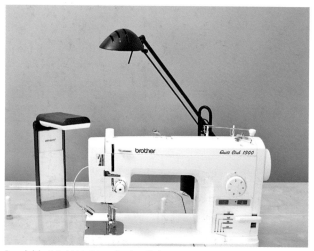

Bendable Bright Light and other lights

SINGLE-HOLE NEEDLE PLATE

A single-hole needle plate will go a long way to help improve stitch quality over the standard needle plate that comes on a machine that does multiple kinds of zigzag and decorative stitches. The single hole helps guide the thread straight up and down as you move the fabric in all different directions. Most sewing machine manufacturers offer a single-hole needle plate as an accessory that can be purchased separately.

Another, and less expensive, solution to this problem is to take an old business card or playing card and poke a small, smooth hole in it and then tape it on the machine table so that the needle goes right through the center of the hole. This will also cover the feed dogs if you have a machine that does not allow you to lower the feed dogs.

Homemade single-hole needle plate

SPARE BOBBIN CASE

If you have a machine that has a standard bobbin case, I suggest that you purchase an extra one that will be dedicated to machine quilting. Put a drop of fingernail polish on it to identify that it is just for machine quilting. I bet your mother told you to never ever touch the little screw on the bobbin case. This is because your mother always used the same top and bottom thread for her sewing. She knew that if you tightened or loosened this screw, it would mess up her stitch quality.

As machine quilters, we often use different threads in our machine, both top and bottom. If you have a spare bobbin case, you can adjust the tension on the bobbin by adjusting the screw on the case. Thread tension will be covered in greater detail on page 17.

MAGNIFICATION

I have worn bifocal glasses for many years and find that I still need additional magnification when I am doing machine quilting. When I was doing machine quilting on a longarm machine for myself and others, I would wear an optical visor to allow me to see better. At home and on the road, when I am working at a sit-down machine, I always wear a pair of half reading glasses over my regular glasses to get the extra magnification that I need. This looks pretty goofy, but I am trying to do quality work, not make a fashion statement to my family and peers. (My family knows I am pretty goofy.)

The glasses are not very strong, about +1.50 magnification. They also work really well if you have to rip any stitches out.

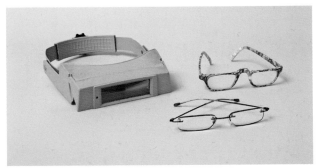

Extra magnification

NEEDLE TO BURY THREADS

If you are one who likes to bury your threads each time you start and end, you will want to invest in some self-threading needles. See pages 20–21 for more details.

Supplies

QUILT TOP

This is your current pride and joy, and you want to make it look as good as possible for its final intended use. Ask yourself: How much time do I want to invest in the machine quilting? Is it a baby quilt that is going to be literally loved to pieces or the next blue-ribbon winner at Houston? The answer to these questions is going to have a tremendous impact on the time you invest in the machine quilting.

BATTING

Once your quilt is finished, the batting is the one thing that you hopefully never see again. I say this because if you elect to use an inexpensive polyester batting, it may come back to haunt you forever. This dreaded occurrence is called bearding. This is when the ends of the fibers start working their way through the top and back of the quilt. If this happens, you will never be able to get rid of them.

Even though the batting is completely enclosed in the quilt, I would not recommend scrimping on quality. My batting preference is Hobbs Heirloom Cotton 80/20 batting. It is 80% cotton and 20% polyester. This batting quilts beautifully, and when your quilt is washed, it will shrink about 3% to give you a nice antique look. If you are making an art quilt and don't want this effect, you might want to preshrink your batting.

There are many types of batting made from different materials with different lofts (thicknesses). Find one that suits your needs and gives you the look that you want, but please do not scrimp on the quality, because you just might regret it.

BACKING FABRIC

Fabric choice for the back is a matter of personal choice, but I want to give you my thoughts on this matter. The back of your quilt will never look as good as the top because of variations in stitch quality caused by needle flex as you sew in different directions. If you change thread colors to match the fabric you are stitching on, as I do, this can be quite distracting on the back. Because of this, I recommend using a small, busy print for the back. This will help to disguise any tension problems and will help mute the thread color changes.

Busy backing prints

PINS

The quilt top, batting, and backing must be securely joined together before you do any machine quilting. The most common method of doing this is to use safety pins. I prefer to use No. 2 pins that are 1½˝ long. I find them easier to put in and remove than smaller ones. This is especially true when you are really focusing on your work and a pin gets jammed under the hopping foot, and believe me, this will happen more than once.

Make sure you purchase good-quality pins that are sharp and will not mar the quilt surfaces with rust or metal oxidation. If you encounter pins that do not easily go through the quilt sandwich, try dragging the shaft of the pin across your scalp. The natural oils in your hair will help lubricate the pin and allow it to easily slide through the fabric and batting.

MASKING TAPE

I use masking or painter's tape in different widths in a variety of ways.

Wider tape (¾˝) can be used to tape the backing fabric to a flat surface so the batting and top can be positioned without having to worry about the backing slipping. I also use ¼˝- and ½˝-wide tapes (along with the ¾˝) as guides for quilting straight or gently curving lines. These narrower-width tapes are available at automotive paint stores. Some quilt shops carry ¼˝-wide quilter's tape. The ½˝ tape is a staple in my box of quilting supplies.

A word of caution about standard masking tape: Do not leave it stuck to your quilt top for extended periods of time. It may become brittle and be very hard to get off. The blue painter's tape is easier to remove, but it does not stick as well as the beige masking tape. Painter's tape also does not come in the narrower widths.

THREAD

Wow! Here is a subject that could fill an entire book in itself. When I started machine quilting, there was not much to choose from, but now there are a tremendous number of different threads to enhance your quilts.

I am going to go over different thread materials, sizes, and uses. Each of us has preferences in terms of the look of our finished quilts, be it traditional or contemporary, and different threads will affect this look.

You might be tempted to buy those bargain-bin threads that you see at some stores. After all, you are going to need several colors, and the thread at quilt shops seems so expensive. My advice is don't do it. If you do succumb, you are asking for, and will get, a lot of frustration.

I have an adage that I try to live by: "You get what you pay for, if you are lucky."

THREAD SIZE AND MEASUREMENT

If it seems confusing when people talk about thread size, that is because it is confusing. Unfortunately, thread manufacturers do not have a standardized method of determining thread size or methods of measurement. It is my guess that this is done on purpose to get you to buy more thread. If you look at thread from three different companies and all of them have a 40 on the spool, you might assume that all three spools are the same size and weight. Chances are you would be wrong. One spool may be marked 40 wt., while the next spool might be marked 40/2, and the third spool could be marked Tex 40. Each of these threads will be a different size and weight. So when you hear someone say they are using a 40-weight thread, they may not know what they are talking about.

What's a quilter to do with these confusing bits of information? The best thing to do, short of using thread from the same manufacturer and product line, is trust your eyes and sense of touch.

Ask yourself, "What do I want my quilting to look like?" If you want the quilting to show up in a bold manner, then you will want to select a larger-diameter thread. This is the look that I prefer because I want my quilting to make as much of a statement as possible. Perhaps you want a more subtle look, or maybe you have not honed your skills just yet and you do not want your little mistakes to be quite so obvious. If that is the case, then you might want to go with a smaller-diameter thread.

The end use of the quilt must also be considered. If the quilt is going to get a lot of heavy use, you probably do not want to use a small, weak thread, but if you are making a wallhanging, this is not going to be as much of a concern.

Thread Content

Threads are most commonly made from cotton, polyester, cotton/polyester, nylon, and rayon. Cotton is a natural fibrous material, polyester and nylon are man-made materials, and rayon is derived from wood.

All threads except monofilament are made from yarn that has been spun from fibers. These yarns are then twisted together in a particular fashion to make the finished thread. The term "ply" refers to the number of individual yarns that have been twisted together. A two-ply thread will have two yarns twisted together, and a three-ply will have three yarns.

Cotton

Cotton thread has always been the gold standard for hand quilters, and when I started machine quilting, I carried this thought for a time. I was told that I must use cotton thread on cotton quilts. Not knowing why, I started asking questions and got the standard answer from most that I talked to: "That's the way it has always been done." I accepted this logic until I talked to my sewing machine service-man, who, along with his brother, had worked in the garment industry for over twenty years. He told me that all clothes are sewn with polyester thread, with no adverse effects on the longevity from mixing fiber types.

Cotton thread is going to give your quilt a more traditional look. Many polyester threads are virtually indistinguishable from cotton thread.

All cotton threads are mercerized. This is a treatment with a caustic liquid to make the thread take dyes better and to give the thread a better luster. High-quality cotton thread is "gassed" during the manufacturing process. This involves passing the thread near a flame to burn off most of the fine fibers that stick out from the thread. Gassing helps give the thread a shiny look.

Polyester

Polyester thread has become enormously popular for machine quilting. This is due in large part to Superior Threads. Bob and Heather Purcell have worked hand in hand with thread manufacturers in Japan to develop a wide variety of threads for quilters. When I first met Bob, about all he had in his product line was gold and silver metallic thread. Now the company has a very wide variety of threads for all types of uses.

Polyester thread can be manufactured so it looks almost identical to cotton thread, or it can be made very shiny so that it looks quite glitzy. When it is shiny, it will give your machine quilting a bright, vibrant look. It is also suitable for machine embroidery. This thread will have the look of silk thread but will be stronger and less expensive.

Cotton-Wrapped Polyester

This thread has a polyester core and a cotton outer wrapping. About all I can say about this type of thread is that I cannot make it work for machine quilting. When I was making garments many years ago, this is the only thread that was available to me, and it worked just fine for that. I know some use it for piecing, but I have gotten rid of all that I had. In the past, when I was desperate for a particular color, I tried to use it for machine quilting, and it was a nightmare.

Rayon

Rayon was developed during World War II because of the shortage of cotton, which was being used in the war effort. This thread is made from cellulose, which comes from wood. Rayon thread will have the look of silk thread and shiny polyester. It too can be used for machine quilting and embroidery; however, it will not be as strong as polyester when compared size for size.

Monofilament

This thread is made from a single strand of either nylon or polyester material. It comes in two colors, clear or smoke. I prefer to use clear in all of my work. To me, it is less noticeable when light hits it than the smoke color. Personally, I am a big fan of monofilament thread. I use it for almost all of my stitch in-the-ditch and outline work. To me, it makes my mistakes less noticeable. Also, when doing stitch in-the-ditch work where the seam allowances are pressed in alternating directions, you do not have to worry if you are sewing in-the-ditch on a light or dark fabric. I also use clear thread in my bobbin. I like the look of the back of the quilt better.

The downside of nylon monofilament is that it will tend to leave stiff, pointy nubs where the threads are cut off. If the quilt is being used as a true quilt for warmth, this can be irritating to the touch. Polyester monofilament will be softer to the touch but tends to be weaker than nylon monofilament.

I find that people either love or hate this thread, with not much middle ground. If my quilts had a different end use, I might have a different opinion on the whole matter, but my quilts never get used as quilts for warmth, but rather as wallhangings and for trunk shows.

CONCLUSION

In the end, it all boils down to choices and availability.

Ask yourself, "Is my quilt traditional or contemporary? What will be the end use of my quilt?"

If your quilt is traditional, you will probably want to use a cotton thread or polyester that looks like cotton. A contemporary quilt would be a great place to use those decorative threads that catch your eye at your local shop or quilt show. However, the threads that you used on your traditional quilt will be equally at home on a contemporary quilt.

End use comes into play when you consider durability. A baby quilt is going to literally be loved to pieces, but we want to keep the pieces together for as long as possible. With that in mind, you are probably not going to want to use a weaker rayon thread for your quilting. A heavier cotton or polyester thread would be more appropriate in this case. A wallhanging could have just about any thread used on it to get the look you want for your viewers.

I would recommend that whatever thread you decide to use, make sure it is of the highest quality that you can get. It will make the whole process of machine quilting that much more enjoyable.

CHAPTER 2

Free-Motion Quilting— The Basics

Backing and Batting

The backing and batting must be larger than the quilt top to allow for any shifting that might occur during pinning, basting, or machine quilting. I suggest that you make the backing and batting 4″ wider and longer than the size of the quilt top. This will give you 2″ on each side of the quilt for any shifting that might occur during the quilting process.

If one width of fabric is not wide enough, you will have to piece the backing. If you do piece the backing, it is best to press the seams open rather than to one side. This will help reduce the bulk of the seams, making them easier to quilt over and less noticeable.

Basting

SAFETY-PIN BASTING

The top, batting, and backing need to be joined together in a sandwich that can be maneuvered through the machine during the quilting process. It is important that the 3 layers be kept from slipping or shifting during the actual quilting process. Pinning with safety pins is the most common way of securing the three layers.

Secure the backing, right side down, to a flat surface with masking tape if you are using the floor, or with tape or clamps if you are using a table. Take care to ensure that there are no wrinkles in the backing after it is secured in place.

Once the backing is secured in place and is wrinkle free, carefully lay the batting on the backing fabric and smooth out any wrinkles. Next, center the quilt top on the other 2 layers.

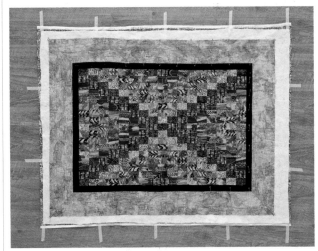

Backing, batting, and top placement

Now that all the layers are in place and are wrinkle free, it is time to pin the 3 layers together. I like to use 1½″-long safety pins, and I place them about every 6″ in each direction. This is different from the norm of putting pins every 3″. It takes half the amount of time to pin at 6″, and there are fewer pins to have to worry about getting jammed in the hopping foot.

I use Collins Crystal Glass Head Pins, C110, to fill in the unpinned space in the immediate area I am quilting. These pins are very small in diameter, and if you should inadvertently sew over them, it is usually not a problem. As I am quilting the quilt, I insert these straight pins only in the immediate area that I am quilting so that I am not constantly getting jabbed by them. I use the machine extension table as a flat surface to make sure that there are no wrinkles in the sandwich when the pins are inserted. Then these pins are removed and reinserted in the next area I am going to quilt.

Combination safety-pin and straight-pin pinning

THREAD BASTING

You might want to see if your local longarm quilter would be willing to machine baste the sandwich together. Have him or her baste a grid with very long stitches, about 3″ on center each direction. This will cost you some money, but it will save you a lot of time in the pinning process and also time while doing the actual quilting because you will not have to deal with any pins.

SPRAY BASTING

Spray basting is another method of securing the layers. I think this is probably acceptable for small projects that are not going to be handled much during the quilting. If you have

to wrestle the sandwich a lot, you may find that the layers tend to come apart. Should that happen, you will still have to add some pins to secure everything together. If you elect to try this, be sure to carefully read and follow the instructions and safety precautions on the label.

Packaging for Quilting

For those of you who previously quilted with your checkbook, this meant bagging or boxing your quilt and shipping it off to your friendly longarm quilter. Now that you have made the decision to save a lot of money and have the satisfaction of completing your project from start to finish, packaging has a completely different meaning.

By packaging, I mean getting your quilt in a manageable configuration that you can get into the throat of your sewing machine.

The most common method is to tightly roll the quilt sandwich halfway up. Start rolling at one edge and roll it up as tightly as possible until you reach the center of the quilt. Secure the rolled portion with clamps.

Clamps can be purchased at quilt shops, or you can use my favorite, the large spring-binder clamps for papers, which can be purchased at office supply stores. The spring clamps are less likely to slip off as you quilt.

Packaged quilt in machine

You will put the roll into the throat of the machine with the unrolled portion hanging out over the end of the machine. This is where a large flat surface to support the unrolled portion of the quilt comes in handy. The more support you have, the easier it will be to maneuver the quilt. With half of the quilt rolled up, you will only have to deal with half of the bulk.

You will begin quilting in the center and quilt the half of the quilt that is rolled up. This means you will be quilting, then unrolling a section, reclamping, and then quilting again until you reach the outside edge of the quilt.

When you reach the outside edge of the quilt, take it out of the machine and roll up the other side and repeat the quilting process.

By quilting in this manner, it will be easier to control the distortion that is created when doing machine quilting. Every stitch we put in our quilt causes a certain amount of distortion when the stitch compresses the top, batting, and back into a thin layer.

I always do all of my stitch in-the-ditch work on the entire quilt first so I know I have everything locked down and secure before doing any motif or background work. I begin stitching in-the-ditch across the center and move out toward the edges. (See page 38 for stitch in-the-ditch information.)

Tension

It is very important to have proper tension when machine quilting. If the bobbin thread tension is too loose or the top thread tension is too tight, the bobbin thread will tend to be pulled to the top of the quilt, and the top thread will lie flat against the quilt top. Conversely, if the bobbin tension is too tight or the top thread tension is too loose, the bobbin thread will lie flat against the back of the quilt, and the top thread will be pulled to the bottom.

Good tension

Top tension too loose or bobbin tension too tight

Top tension too tight or bobbin tension too loose

Threads are made from different materials and come in different diameters. These variables affect how the thread flows off the bobbin, and this ultimately has an effect on tension and stitch quality.

TOP OR SPOOL TENSION

This is one place the tension can be adjusted on machines with standard bobbin cases. It is the only place tension can be easily adjusted on machines with a drop-in bobbin.

Many machines have a knob on the front of the machine to adjust tension.

note:

To adjust the tension, just remember this old saying: "lefty-loosey and righty-tighty."

Most of the new electronic machines have a menu that will allow you to adjust the tension by tapping the screen. If you have a menu to tap, generally the higher the number, the tighter the tension will be.

BOBBIN TENSION

A good starting point for bobbin tension is doing what is called the yo-yo test. To do this, remove your bobbin and case from the machine and, with the bobbin still in the case, hold the thread between your thumb and forefinger. Dangle the bobbin case in the air and gently bounce it up and down. If the bobbin and case fall to the ground, the tension is too loose.

Yo-yo test

If they do not drop at all, the tension is too tight. The case should drop just slightly each time you bounce it.

The bobbin also uses the "lefty-loosey and righty-tighty" adjustment method.

This is just a starting point, and further adjustments may have to be made as you check your actual stitch quality.

STITCH QUALITY

One of the biggest challenges in machine quilting is maintaining a good stitch quality. I wish there was a simple solutions to this constant source of frustration, but there isn't.

When machine quilting, we are doing something that a sewing machine is not designed to do. Without getting too technical, I will try to describe what is going on when you are piecing and when you are machine quilting. When piecing, the feed dogs, needle, and hook (the pointy thing that makes the stitch) have a distinct mechanical relationship with one another. Everything works in harmony, and all is good.

However, when we are machine quilting, there are no feed dogs to move the fabric through the machine, just our hands. Our hands move in all different directions as we move the project through the machine, and there is no mechanical relationship between our hands and the position of the needle at any one time. If we are moving our hands at a constant speed all of the time, that means there is constant pressure on the needle in the direction we are moving the fabric. Consequently, the needle is being flexed away from the hook, except when we are going straight forward or backward. This flexing will cause our stitch quality to be degraded as we change directions when quilting.

Well, you're probably saying to yourself that this sounds pretty hopeless. There are, however, a few things you can do to make the best of this bad situation. The first thing is to test stitch quality on a scrap of the same fabric, batting, and backing that you are going to quilt on. Stitch in all different directions on your test piece. Now, look at both sides and check the stitch quality. You will probably see that when you are going straight forward or backward, your stitches look quite good. When you start going at an angle, a curve, or in a circle, that is when the stitches start to look bad, with either the top or the bobbin thread lying almost flat against the surface of the fabric. This is where the needle is flexing away from the hook and the tension is disrupted.

PROBLEM

The bobbin thread lies flat on the back, or the top thread is visible on the back in the form of dots at the beginning and end of each stitch.

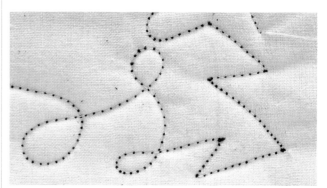

Top tension is too loose; back of quilt.

Solution

Increase the top tension or reduce the bobbin tension and retest.

Use a larger-diameter needle.

Caution

If you increase the tension too much, you will see the top thread lying flat against the fabric. This is kind of like walking a tightrope, so make your adjustments in small increments.

PROBLEM

The top thread lies flat on the top, or the bobbin thread is visible on the top in the form of dots at the beginning and end of each stitch.

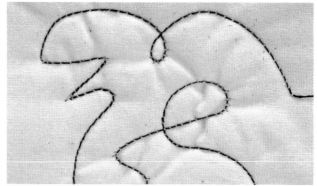

Top tension is too tight; front of quilt.

Solution

Decrease the top tension or increase the bobbin tension.

Use a larger needle.

Caution

If you adjust the tension too much, you will see the bobbin thread lying flat on the back.

Your stitch quality will never look as good as it does when you are piecing. I want the top of my quilt to look as good as possible; this is the "art" to me. The back of my piece is the back, and that is all it is. Of course, I am going to try to get stitches as good as possible on both sides, but if there is any sacrificing in stitch quality to be done, I will do it on the back. I liken a quilt to a fine art painting. I never take a painting I like off someone's wall and look at the back of the canvas.

Another trick I do to make the back look as good as possible is to use a small, busy print for the backing fabric. The small, busy print makes it difficult to see any problems that might have occurred while stitching. A busy print in conjunction with a very fine blending colored thread or monofilament thread will also help improve the appearance of the back of the quilt.

Starting and Finishing a Quilting Design

When you start and finish a quilting design, you must secure the top and bottom threads together, so that they will not unravel as time goes by. There are a few different ways of doing this chore, and I will discuss them, along with the pros and cons of each.

note:

Many of the newer machines come equipped with an automatic thread cutter. This feature is wonderful for piecing but not so good for machine quilting. I recommend not using the thread cutter when machine quilting because you cannot pull up the bobbin thread when you start out on a quilting design. Yes, I admit that the machine will pick up the thread, but you will probably end up with a big, unsightly knot on the back of your quilt.

METHOD 1: STITCHING IN ONE PLACE

To use this technique, bring the bobbin thread to the top of the quilt at the beginning of a quilting design.

1. Lower the presser foot and grasp the top thread between the thumb and forefinger of your left hand.

2. Put a slight amount of tension on the thread by gently pulling on the thread.

3. While you have the thread under tension, turn the hand-wheel toward you with your right hand. As the needle goes through the cycle of making a stitch, the bobbin thread will be pulled to the top of the quilt sandwich because of the tension that you have been putting on the top thread.

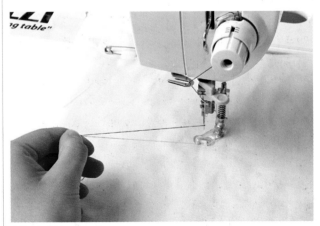

Bring bobbin thread to top.

4. Hold both threads between your thumb and fore-finger, again with a slight amount of tension on both threads. Take 3 or 4 stitches in one place to secure the top and bottom threads together in a "knot."

5. The thread ends can be clipped off close to the quilt surface or buried using a hand-sewing needle later on. If you are going to clip them off, wait until you have started the design and the needle is away from the loose threads. When you get to the end of the design, you will once again stitch in place to knot the threads. Again, the threads will be clipped off or worked in later.

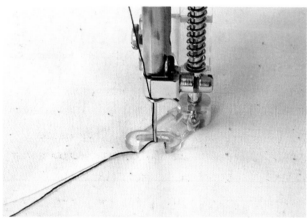
Stitch in place to knot threads.

METHOD 2: BACKSTITCHING

Another way of starting and finishing a design is to back-stitch at the beginning and end of a design. Starting and stopping will be more visible on the top of the quilt with this method than with the other two methods.

1. Pull the threads up (Steps 1–3, page 19), but bring them up about ³⁄₁₆″ from the start of the design on the line of the design.

2. Backstitch to the beginning of the design and then stitch over the backstitching to lock the threads together.

3. Do the same thing at the end by stitching to the end of the design and then backstitching about ³⁄₁₆″ over what you have already stitched.

4. Finish the loose threads off as before (Steps 4–5, at left).

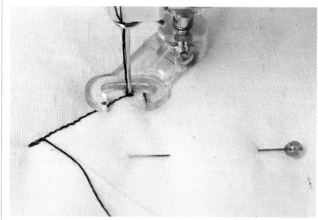
Backstitch to secure threads.

METHOD 3: KNOTTING BY TYING

The last method of starting and stopping looks the most professional but also takes the most time to do. It's funny how that always seems to be the case, isn't it? If you use this method of pulling the threads to the back, tying them, and burying them between the layers, you will need to start stitching one stitch before the start of the design and go one stitch beyond the end of the design, because you will lose a stitch at each end when you pull the threads to the back.

1. When you start stitching, pull the threads up (Steps 1–3, page 19), but immediately start stitching without doing any knotting or backstitching.

2. When you have completed stitching, pull the threads at the beginning and end of the stitched design to the back, tie the ends in a square knot, and then bury the threads in the batting between the top and the back using a hand-sewing needle. This can be done after each design is finished or after the entire quilt is completed. Be warned: if you wait too long to knot and bury the threads, you may have a real mess on your hands because there will be so many threads to deal with.

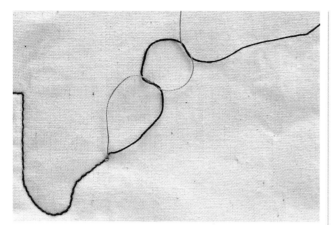

Tie a square knot.

You can use a self-threading needle to speed up the process some, but it is still pretty time-consuming.

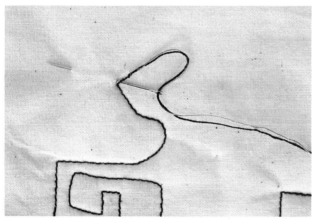

Bury threads.

Hand Placement

Hand placement is very important when machine quilting. I like to think of my hands as an embroidery hoop that moves the quilt sandwich through the machine.

tip

In fact, it is possible to put the sandwich in a hoop or lay a hoop on top of the quilt and then hold onto it as you move the quilt sandwich.

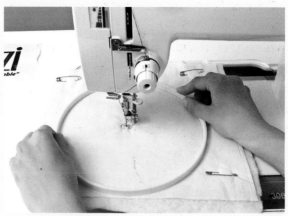

Using embroidery hoop

If you place your hands on both sides of the needle, you will have much better control than if you place your hands at the edge of the extension table.

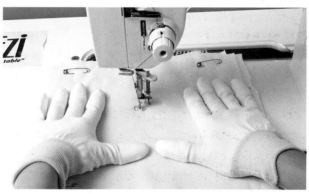

Good hand placement

Adjust the position of your hands depending on which direction you will be stitching. If you know that you are going to be stitching from left to right, for example, when you start stitching, place your right hand as close to the needle as possible, leaving extra space between your left hand and the needle. This will give you a larger range of motion. Keep in mind that you are going to be starting and stopping many times, so the farther you can go between times when you have to move your hands, the more efficient you will be in the long run.

Practice Exercise

Complete the following exercise to learn the basics of machine quilting. This is not nearly as hard to do as you might think. You have to start somewhere, and it might as well be at the beginning.

1. Install a hopping foot (see page 6) and lower or cover the feed dogs. For learning purposes only, put a dark-colored thread on the top and a light-colored thread in the bobbin. The thread color variation will be quite informative for stitch quality evaluation.

Machine set up for free-motion quilting

2. Layer 2 pieces of muslin about 12″ × 12″ with a piece of batting between them. Use 4 or 5 safety pins to hold everything together.

12″ × 12″ practice piece

3. Set the machine in the needle-down position, if possible, and insert the practice piece under the needle.

Practice piece in machine

4. Pull the bobbin thread up and secure the threads together (see page 19).

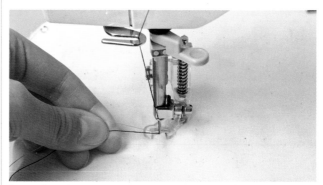

Secure threads.

tip

*Make sure you lower the presser foot. It is very **easy** to forget to do this, and it will lead to disastrous results. The top will look just fine, but the bottom will be horrible.*

Forgot to lower presser foot

5. Put your hands in the proper position (see page 21) and begin stitching.

6. Press on the foot pedal and begin moving the fabric with your hands.

note:

If you do not move the fabric after the machine has taken 3 or 4 stitches, the thread will probably break, and you will have to start over again.

All I want you to do right now is doodle with the machine and fabric. Just get the feel of moving the fabric in different directions with your hands acting as the feed dogs. Pretend that you are a child again, and you are drawing with a pencil and paper. Now the pencil is the needle of the machine, and the paper is the practice panel. The only difference is that instead of moving the pencil, you are now moving the paper.

This is not meant to be a fast process. I tend to go at a pretty slow pace. There are some instructors who will tell you that you must run the machine at full speed and just get used to the fast pace. I feel that this will lead to a lot of frustration because you are always out of control. Try to go just fast enough that you are not making jerky movements. The faster you can go and still maintain control, the smoother your stitching will be. It won't be long before you will develop a comfortable working pace. Just remember: this isn't a race.

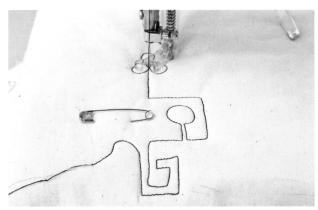

Doodling

You can't easily lift the pencil off the paper to start another drawing, but here's how to easily move from one design to another.

Secure the threads at the end of the design you have just finished stitching (see page 20, Step 4). Rather than clipping the threads and moving to the next design and starting over by bringing up the bobbin thread like when you first started, try this: raise the needle and hopping foot, then slide the quilt sandwich over to the next design, secure the threads, and begin stitching again.

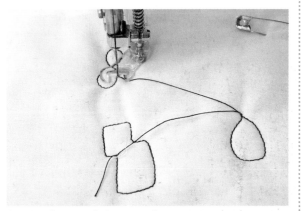

Jumping from one design to another

This little time-saving trick will be difficult to do if you are starting and ending your stitching by tying the threads in a knot and then burying them in the batting, but it will work fine for the other two methods of securing the threads. You can clip the threads while you are watching TV in the evening.

Now that you have done some doodling and have gotten the feel for moving the fabric, I want you to jump over to an open area on your practice panel and stitch your name in cursive. You can use the jump trick to cross any t's or dot any i's. It's not nearly as hard as it sounds.

Potential Problem with Stitch Quality, Probable Cause, and Solution

Now that you have spent a little time on the basic exercise of doodling while getting the feel of moving fabric through the machine in different directions, it is time to take a look at your stitch quality. Take your practice piece out of the machine, turn it over, and look at the stitches on the back. There is better than a fifty-fifty chance that the quality of the stitches on the back leaves a little to be desired.

The stitches on the back rarely look as good as the ones on the top because of the fact that the fabric is being moved in different directions, rather than forward or backward, as in regular piecing. When machine quilting, we are doing something with the machine that it is not designed to do. By making a few simple adjustments, you should be able to get the stitches looking pretty darn good.

PROBLEM

Dark dots appear on the back, and the bobbin thread lies flat against the back when you have stitched a curved design.

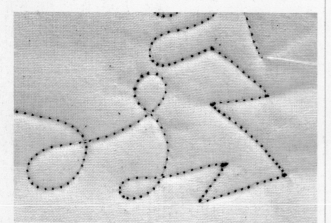

Dark dots and bobbin thread lying flat on back

Cause

The top tension is too loose, or the bobbin tension is too tight. The needle may be flexing excessively.

Solution

If you have not already done so, replace the needle with a size 14 or 16 needle.

Try tightening the top tension (see page 17). After making this adjustment, stitch some more doodles and then look at the stitches on the back again. Continue tightening the top tension until you're happy with the stitches.

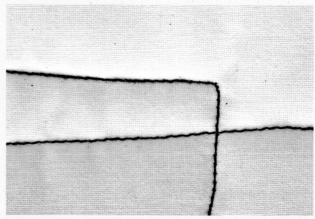

Correct tension

If you were to continue to tighten the top tension, eventually you would see the bobbin thread being pulled to the top of your quilt and the thread from the spool would lie flat on the top. If this happens, it is then time to loosen the top tension slightly to achieve the perfect balance.

This is going to be a constant balancing act as you machine quilt. Thread type, diameter, and even color will have an effect on stitch quality. I think you will find that red and black threads are among the most difficult to use. I believe that this is a function of the dyes that are used in these threads.

I recommend that you always have a practice panel by your machine, and every time you change threads, do some doodling and make tension adjustments before getting back to work on your prize-winning quilt.

Potential Problems with Stitch Length, Probable Causes, and Solutions

I am commonly asked what the proper stitch length is. Unfortunately, I can't give you a definitive answer to this question. You are the artist, and you should strive to have a stitch length that is pleasing to you. I will tell you that I like to have my stitches close to the same length as my machine's default stitch, which I use for piecing.

While working on the practice pieces that you will be doing in this book, I want you to do one thing: concentrate on making your stitches a consistent length all the time. If you can make them all pretty close to the same length, then I can tell you what you need to do to get them to the length that pleases you.

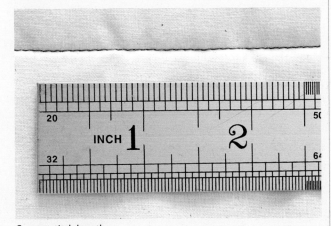

Correct stitch length

PROBLEM

A very common problem students face when they begin machine quilting is that their stitches are too short.

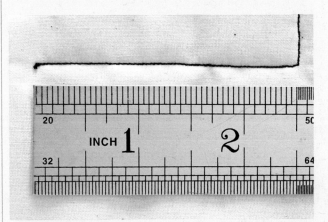

Stitches too short

Cause

Moving your hands too slowly in relation to the speed of the needle going up and down causes small stitches.

Solution

To lengthen your stitches, you have two variables you can adjust. You can either speed up your hands or slow the speed of the needle. All too often, when I tell my students to slow the needle speed, they slow both the speed of their hands and the speed of the needle. This does not lead to any change in the stitch length, because they have changed both variables at the same time. It is almost as if their hands are connected to their feet; move one, and the other follows suit. You must change only one variable at a time to notice any change in the stitch length.

Concentrate on finding a hand speed that you are comfortable with. You should easily figure this out after a very short amount of time spent practicing. I think you will find that if you move your hands too fast, you will feel out of control and will not be able to follow a marked design with any degree of accuracy. However, if you are moving your hands very slowly, your movements will probably be jerky.

So when you find the speed that you're comfortable with, you can begin to adjust the speed of the needle to adjust the stitch length. In this case, you would slow down the needle speed to lengthen the stitch.

I suggest that you always machine quilt with your shoe removed. You will have more control over the speed of the machine because you will be able to feel the pedal better. In addition, I recommend that you put your entire foot on the pedal. You will have better leverage with the whole foot on the pedal, not just the ball of your foot.

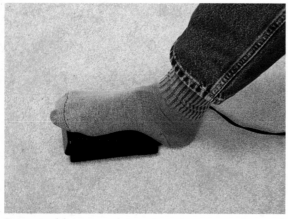

Foot on pedal

PROBLEM

Having stitches that are too long is another common problem.

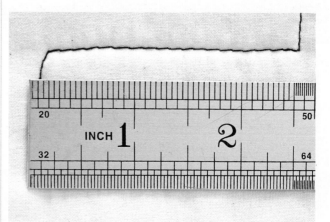

Stitches too long

Cause

Moving your hands too fast in relation to the speed of the needle going up and down causes large stitches.

Solution

To shorten the stitch length, you have the same two variables to adjust as when the stitches were too short. You can get your stitches shorter by either slowing your hands down or making the needle go up and down faster. Do not adjust both variables at the same time. Use the table below as a quick guide to adjust stitch length.

Adjust Either, Not Both	To Get Longer Stitches	To Get Shorter Stitches
Hand Speed	Faster	Slower
Needle Speed	Slower	Faster

Bad Habits to Avoid

If you can avoid these habits from the beginning, you will be better off in the long run.

■ Do not spin your practice piece if you are stitching a circle or loop. You can get away with this on these small practice pieces, but when you start working on larger pieces, it will be impossible to get the quilt through the throat of the machine; practice moving the quilt in a circular motion without actually spinning the quilt.

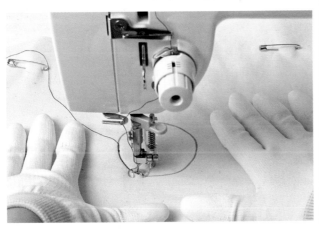

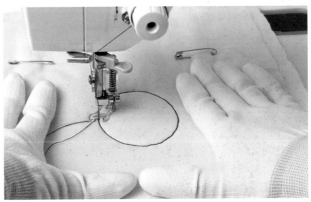

Stitching a circle

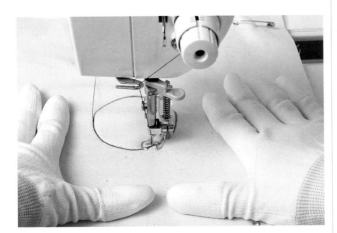

■ Do not lift your hands while the machine is running. It is very tempting to try to reposition your hands while the machine is running, but if you do, you will notice that you may have a few stitches that go off track. At the very least, you will have a few stitches longer or shorter than before you moved your hands. Be sure to let the machine come to a complete stop before moving your hands. Just because you took your foot off the pedal doesn't mean that the machine will instantly stop. If you have told the machine to stop with the needle in the down position, it will go through the cycle until it gets to the down position.

Continue to practice doodling until you start to become comfortable with moving the fabric in different directions and you are starting to get the hang of getting your stitches the same length. Just remember: your skill level is a function of practice, practice, practice. Do you know what you need to do when you are sick and tired of practicing? *Practice some more!*

CHAPTER 3

Learning to Draw and Stitch Designs

In the last chapter you learned the basics of how to move your quilt sandwich through the machine with the feed dogs down and how to stitch in different directions without rotating the fabric.

It is assumed that by now you are at least somewhat comfortable with this process. If you are like me, you probably skimmed over the last chapter and decided to get right to the fun stuff. That is exactly what I usually do, and more often than not, I end up having a lot of frustration. (It is a good thing, I think, that I am a very stubborn and determined person.)

That being said, if you are not comfortable with the concept of doodling and stitching in different directions, I urge you to go back and practice some more. You probably have noticed that I am somewhat of a nag about the practicing thing.

I am going to raise the bar in this chapter by having you stitch on lines rather than just going willy-nilly in any direction. You will probably find this somewhat frustrating at first, but if you promise to not get discouraged, I am sure I can work you through the process.

Force yourself to blink your eyes quite often. This simple exercise will help keep your eyes lubricated, and this will help reduce eyestrain.

Practice Exercise

Use the basic shapes and designs on pages 43–47 to design a panel to practice stitching on lines.

You can also use common things you have around the house: cookie cutters, plates, saucers, cups, small boxes, and a straightedge to easily duplicate the designs provided or to make your own designs.

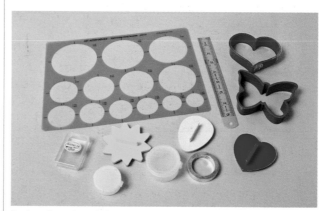

Designs from found objects

At this point it is not important how pretty or uniform your designs are. All we are concerned with is developing control over the quilt sandwich.

1. Cut a piece of muslin the width of the bolt by 36″ long. Leave the piece folded in half as it came off the bolt, and press if necessary to remove any wrinkles.

2. Draw a series of designs on the muslin. Start with straight lines, squares, triangles, curves, and so forth. You can use anything to mark these designs. A pencil, ball-

point pen, or marking pen will work just fine. All you need is to be able to see the markings.

Do not worry about the quality or accuracy of the designs. We are going to practice control and following the lines.

3. Place a piece of thin batting between the layers of folded muslin. Use safety pins to pin the sandwich together. Put the pins about 6˝ apart, trying to keep the pins away from the lines you have drawn.

Sandwiched and pinned practice panel

4. Put a color of thread on the machine that will contrast strongly with the marking color and the color of the muslin. Use a thread in the bobbin that contrasts with the thread on the spool for this exercise. Try to stay away from red and black threads, as they can cause problems going through the machine. (I used black thread in the photos seen throughout the book for maximum visibility. On a real quilt I would never use 2 different thread colors.)

5. Using the skills developed in Chapter 2, stitch along the lines of the designs you marked in Step 2 above. Start with the straight lines and simple shapes and work your way up to the more complex designs.

You will probably notice right away that trying to follow lines is much harder to do than the simple doodling was. Do not despair; you will improve dramatically with just a little practice.

It is my guess that your stitch length has also gotten much shorter when compared with the doodling that you were previously doing. This is to be expected

because you are now intently concentrating on stitching right on the lines to the best of your ability. The stitches are shorter because you are moving your hands more slowly than before. As you become more confident, you will find you can move your hands faster, which will lengthen your stitches.

Following these designs is going to force you to stitch in different directions because you can't spin the quilt.

6. After stitching a few designs, take your practice panel out of the machine and spend a couple of minutes evaluating your stitch quality in relation to thread tension. This is a great time to make adjustments and then evaluate the changes you have made as you continue practicing. The contrasting thread colors will help you evaluate the changes made.

When you are beginning to learn to machine quilt, you will no doubt be intently looking at the needle going up and down. This will cause your eyes to become tired quite quickly. With practice, your skill level will increase, and you will be able to look at where you are going and not so much at where you are right now.

Below I have listed some of the more common problems you are probably experiencing. Take a break from your stitching practice and review them with your practice panel in front of you. I have been teaching machine quilting for many years, and these are the problems students have over and over again.

After reviewing the problems, causes, and solutions, I would like you to take a break for a couple of hours or even overnight. When you come back to start again, either change the thread color of the spool or mark another practice panel and begin stitching again, keeping in mind the solutions to the problems that I believe you are having. You can certainly work on all of the problems you are having at once, but it might be a good idea to pick one at a time and overcome the problems individually.

Potential Problems with Stitching on the Lines, Probable Causes, and Solutions

I wish I were with you to evaluate your work and help you with any problems that you might be having, but unfortunately, I am not. The next best thing I can do is to list some common problems that my students encounter when they start out. These problems happen over and over with each new class I teach.

Included with each problem in the section below will be a probable cause or causes and a suggested solution.

I think it is about time for a little pep talk from Mr. Quilt. I would guess that if you are a true beginner, you are getting a bit frustrated and discouraged about now. You might even be thinking about giving up and going back to quilting with your checkbook. Please do not be discouraged. This is not an easy skill to learn, but you can learn it if you will just stick with it. I like to say to my students, "If it were easy to do, then everybody would be doing it."

PROBLEM

Inability to follow the lines

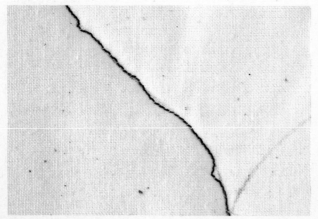

Stitching off lines

Possible Causes

Inexperience, poor lighting, poor visibility, and/or your hands are slipping

Solution

Practice some more by changing thread color and going back over the designs again and again. Stop when you get tired of practicing, take a break, and then practice some more. There is nothing magical about this process. All you need to do is identify your problems and practice eliminating them. Notice how I use the dirty "p" word over and over again?

Make sure you have extra lighting directed at the needle area. Most sewing machines do not have a bright enough light to adequately illuminate this area. I recommend an external source to really direct light to the needle area. The Bendable Bright Light is one of my favorites. It is very bright and can be directed right where I need it. It has another advantage in that it does not put out very much heat (page 10).

As I have gotten older, I find that my eyes are not what they used to be, and they were never very good to begin with. To compensate for this, I always wear a pair of half reading glasses over my bifocal glasses (page 11).

The hopping foot creates a blind spot at times, so you will be unable to see your design. When this occurs, twist your quilt sandwich about 20°–30° to the left or right so you can see what you are doing. By doing this, you should be able to see well enough behind the needle and hopping foot to stitch the part of the design that has been blocked by the foot. Twist the quilt back into its original orientation when you have cleared this area.

It is imperative that you have a good grip, but at the same time a light touch on your work while moving it through the machine. An in-depth discussion of traction devices begins on page 7.

PROBLEM

Long or erratic stitches when you start stitching

Long or erratic stitches

Possible Causes

It is very difficult to get the machine up to the proper speed and at the same time get your hands moving at the correct speed. Actually, I would say that it is impossible to do. In your haste to get up to speed with both variables in play, you will probably have a few bad stitches.

Solution

Before you start moving your hands and the quilt, try getting your machine up to speed. This means you will take 2 or 3 stitches in one place while the machine is coming up to speed. As you are doing this, talk to yourself and say, "Stitch, stitch, move." I think you will find that doing only one thing at a time will help to eliminate those long and/or erratic stitches. The fact that you are taking a couple of stitches in one place will not make any difference and will hardly be noticeable at all.

PROBLEM

Erratic or long stitches while stitching

Possible Causes

You only have a certain range of motion when you are machine quilting. Because of this, you will have to stop and reposition your hands many times. There is a good chance, as a beginner, that you may be changing the position of your hands while the machine is running. You are probably concentrating so hard on what you are doing that you are unaware of this action. When you pick up your hands and reposition them while the machine is running, it is very easy to jostle your work and disrupt the stitch pattern.

Another potential cause is not keeping the machine running at a constant speed. If the machine speed goes up and down while your hands are moving at a constant speed, your stitches will vary in length.

Erratic hand speed will also create erratic stitch lengths.

Solution

When you have reached the limit of your range of motion, lift your foot off the pedal. Just because you lift your foot does not mean that the machine will instantly stop. Be sure to wait for the machine to come to a complete stop before you pick up your hands. If you have the machine set to stop in the needle-down position, it will continue through its cycle until it gets to that position.

If you can see that you will be primarily moving the quilt from left to right, try this little trick. Place your right hand as close to the needle as is safely possible and your left hand as far away from the needle as is comfortably possible. Be sure to still keep your hands in a position so they are straddling the needle and not at the bottom of your work table. By doing this, you will be able to move your work farther than if you had centered the needle between your hands when you started out. Likewise, if you will be moving the quilt away from you, try starting out with your arms alongside your chest so you are able to reach farther before you have to stop and move your hands.

Some of the newer machines have a speed control built in. This means that the machine will not run any faster than where it is set, no matter how hard you press on the pedal. This is a nice feature that helps control one variable, but it is not a necessity. My machines do not have this feature, and I really do not think I would use it if I had it.

Try to develop the habit of moving your hands as fast as you can while still maintaining control over your accuracy. The faster you can go, the smoother your stitching will be, especially on curves and circles. Consistent hand speed is strictly a function of practicing and practicing some more. Be aware that it is a common tendency to go faster when stitching a curve or circle. I think this is because we want to get through this part as quickly as possible and get on to some easy straight lines.

PROBLEM

Inability to see behind the needle area

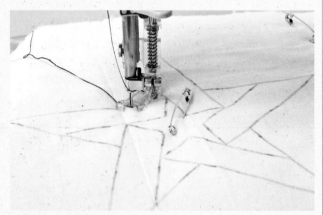

Blind spot behind needle

Cause

Well, this one is pretty obvious. The needle shaft and hopping foot create a blind spot for all of us. In theory you can machine quilt without a hopping foot if you are able to hold the quilt sandwich flat against the machine bed. The only problem with this is that at some point you will probably sew through one of your fingers. I am sorry for the lack of a photograph on this one, but I think you get the idea. Granted, you would probably only do it once, but I do not think it is worth the risk.

Solution

There is no real solution that will eliminate the blind spot behind the needle shaft and hopping foot. I suggest that you rotate (twist) your work about 20°–30° one way or the other so you can better see what you are doing.

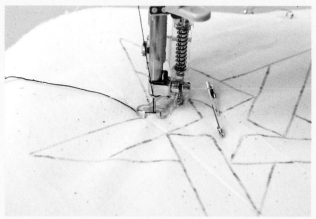

Rotate work.

There is another possibility to get around this problem, although it is a bit cumbersome. You could put your work in a shallow embroidery hoop and then remove the hopping foot. This will keep your work flat against the machine table, and it cannot flop up and down if the hopping foot is removed. By holding onto the hoop, you will be less likely to sew through your finger. You will have to constantly move the hoop as you progress. The hoop should be large enough to allow the quilting of the whole design motif at once. Unfortunately, the throat of the machine is also a limiting factor in the whole process.

Hooped quilt with hopping foot removed

You might also try just pressing one ring of the hoop against the top of the quilt and using it to hold down the quilt as you guide it through the stitching process. This would also eliminate the need for gloves.

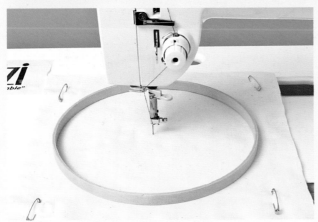

Hoop on top of quilt with hopping foot removed

PROBLEM

Rounded points or V's of designs

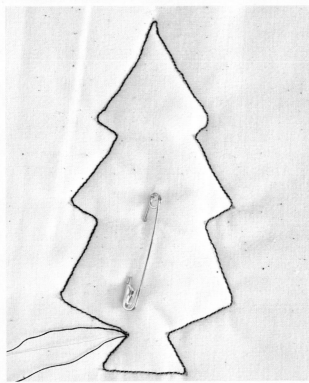

Rounded points or V's

Possible Cause

If you are stitching a design with sharp points or V's, like a star, you may notice that sometimes they are rounded or chopped off. Even though you are following the design exactly, what is probably happening is that as

you approach the point or V, the needle is beginning its upward cycle. When the quilt is moved to where the needle will intersect the point or V, the needle is still coming up or just beginning to go down. By the time the needle pierces the fabric, you have moved beyond the point or V and have started down the other side of the design. This causes the chopped-off or rounded look.

Solution

When you come to the sharp change in direction, pause at the point or V and take 2 stitches. That way you can be assured of having a nice, crisp design. Once again, say to yourself, "Stitch, stitch" at the point or V. The 2 stitches in one place will not be at all noticeable. As you get more proficient with your stitching, you will probably be able to cut this down to one stitch, but you must stay alert and not get lazy.

Isn't It Time You Were a Movie Star?

Like it or not, we are all living in the techno era. There are many gadgets designed to make our lives easier and more interesting. I am not totally convinced about some of them, but there is one thing I think could help you a lot. That gizmo is a video recorder. Many of us have a digital video recorder, and still more of us have a cell phone or camera that will take videos. If you have one or have a friend who has one, arrange to have videos taken of you while you are actually machine quilting. If the old saying "A picture is worth a thousand words" is true, then a video must be worth at least a million words. While you are machine quilting, you are going to be doing some things you are not conscious of. If you have video images of what is happening, you will be able to see exactly what is going wrong. You will be able to refer back to this chapter and other parts of this book to find a solution for your problem. The other advantage of doing this, as opposed to having me there looking over your shoulder, is that you do not have to listen to me nag you. My wife says that is a blessing in itself.

Ropes, Feathers, and Beyond

Now that you have had a chance to practice stitching the simple designs and evaluate any problems that might have arisen, it is time to begin working on more complicated designs, such as ropes and feathers.

In order to stitch these designs, you will need to practice and perfect one more exercise before moving on.

PRACTICE EXERCISE

1. Draw about 6 of the designs shown below onto a piece of muslin and layer with batting and backing. I liken these designs to blades of grass blowing in the wind.

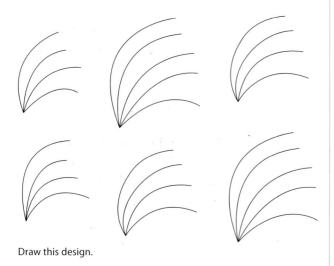

Draw this design.

2. Using a dark-colored thread in both the top and bobbin, stitch continuously from the point where all of the lines meet to the end of one line and then back, directly on top of the line you just stitched.

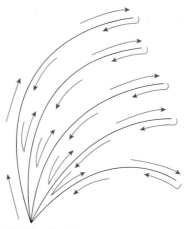

Stitching direction map

3. Repeat this process with each of the other lines. I know this sounds impossible to do, but you will be surprised at how quickly you will catch on to this essential skill. Continue with this exercise until you can consistently stitch back over where you have just stitched. You will be amazed at your improvement as you stitch the 6 designs.

ROPE BORDER

Now we are going to work on a rope border design. When doing ropes, feathers, and for that matter, any other complicated design, the previous exercise will prove to be invaluable.

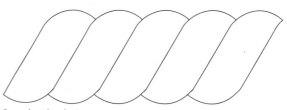

Rope border design

1. Take another piece of muslin about 20″ × 36″ and lightly draw 2 parallel lines, about 3″ apart, the length of the piece of muslin.

3″

Draw parallel lines.

2. Use a 30°–60°–90° triangle and draw a diagonal line between the parallel lines. Use the bottom line as a guide for the triangle.

Draw diagonal line.

3. Draw more diagonal lines, making sure they are equally spaced about 1½˝ apart.

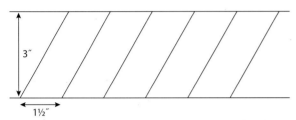

Draw equally spaced diagonal lines.

4. Draw a partial circle with a diameter of about 2˝ on each side of the diagonal lines to complete the rope design. Make sure the partial circle just touches the parallel lines and the diagonal lines.

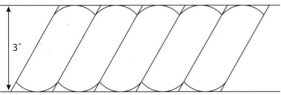

Draw partial circles.

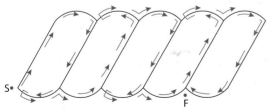

Stitching direction guide; S = Start; F = Finish

5. Use the arrows on the stitching direction guide (above) to see which direction to stitch. It may be helpful to actually draw these arrows onto the rope that you just drew onto the piece of muslin. I will often do this when I am stitching a design for the first time. Notice that the top and bottom of every other rope section is double stitched. The only difference is that it is the sections that are adjacent to the double-stitched top sections that are double stitched. This is where the skill developed from the practice exercise on page 34 will be helpful.

6. Now repeat that exercise using a thread on the spool and in the bobbin that matches the color of the muslin fabric. I think you will be very pleased with your progress, and we are just getting started!

All ropes, feathers, and, for that matter, all complicated designs are basically stitched in the same manner. You will always have to do some backtracking on more complicated designs to be able to complete them in a continuous fashion.

It is important to practice stitching the rope design until you can consistently do it well before moving on to the other designs.

DOUBLE-VEINED FEATHER

The next design we will be working on is the double-veined feather. By double veined I mean that there are 2 lines running down the center of the feather. You could also call this the spine of the feather.

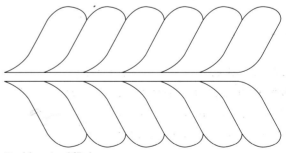

Double-veined feather

Look at the rope and the feather side by side. You will see that each side of the feather is identical to the rope, with one exception. The difference is that the inside edge of the feather is flat, and the bottom of the rope is curved. Other than that minor difference, they are basically the same, and hence they will be stitched in exactly the same manner.

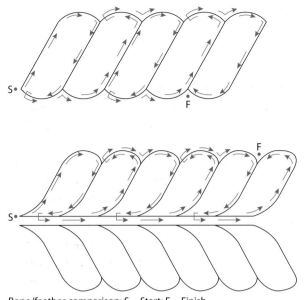

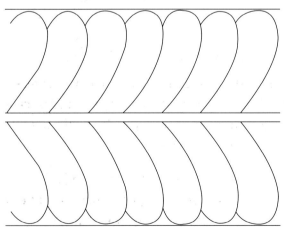

Rope/feather comparison; S = Start; F = Finish

1. Draw 4 parallel lines on your piece of muslin, each pair about 3″ apart (Step 1, page 35), to represent the inside and outside boundaries of the double-veined feather.

2. Refer to Steps 2–4, page 35, and sketch a double-veined feather between these boundaries. Do not worry about making your sketch perfect; just try to make your lines smooth and flowing. All we are trying to do here is to develop control and learn the process of stitching complicated designs.

Sketch double-veined feather.

Both sides of the feather are stitched in exactly the same way. Use the arrows as a stitching guide to quilt this design.

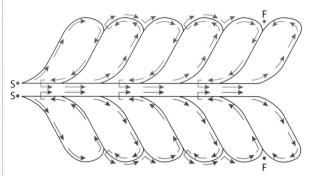

Double-veined feather stitching guide for both sides; S = Start; F = Finish

SINGLE-VEINED FEATHER

A single-veined feather has only one line going down the center of the design.

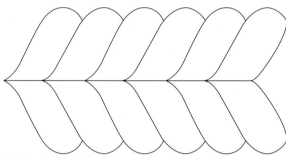

Single-veined feather

1. Draw 3 parallel lines, each about 3″ apart, on your muslin (Step 1, page 35).

2. Refer to Steps 2–4, page 35, and sketch a single-veined feather between these boundaries.

To reduce the amount of stitching required for this design, it will be stitched just a little differently from the rope or the double-veined feather. Two separate passes will be required to stitch this design.

3. For the first pass, start stitching at the pointed end (S).

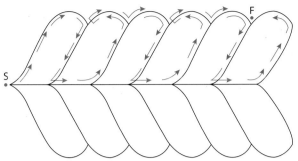

Stitching direction guide for one pass

4. Every time you come to the vein, stitch forward. You will be doing no backstitching on the vein of the feather. This will reduce the amount of double, and sometimes triple, stitching on the vein of the feather.

5. When you reach the end of the design (F), knot and cut the thread.

You could just start back on the other side of the feather. The problem, especially when you are a beginner, is that you have to think backward when stitching. I can do this equally well going both directions, but I always seem more comfortable in going back to the beginning of the design. Another thing I have noticed is that I am more comfortable going from left to right. I think this may be a function of reading and writing left to right my whole life.

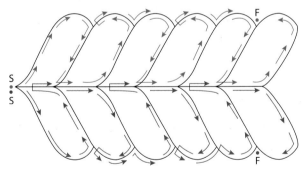

Stitching direction guide for the second pass

6. Return to the starting point (S) and stitch the other side of the feather, ending at the second F. On this pass do the required double stitching on the vein to complete the design.

Other Complicated Designs

When you approach other complicated designs, keep in mind how you stitched the rope and feathers. Use that knowledge to stitch the designs on pages 43 and 45.

Sketch these designs on muslin layered with batting, and practice stitching them. It is not important how pretty or accurate your drawings are at this point; just try to keep the lines smooth. You need to become comfortable navigating your way around all types of designs, with a minimum of stopping and cutting the thread. If it helps you, do not be afraid to draw arrows on the muslin to indicate the stitching direction.

If you miss something when stitching the designs and you do not notice it until you are done, do not worry about it. Just go back and fill that area in and call it good. No one will ever know the difference if you don't tell.

Now is a good time to get those cookie cutters out of storage and put them to work in a low-calorie fashion. Trace around the cutters to make your own designs. Try to make them increasingly complicated so you will have to do some backstitching to complete them. I have given you some sample designs on pages 45 and 47.

Stitch In-The-Ditch

Most of my students use a walking foot to stitch in-the-ditch (SITD). This is the most commonly accepted practice. But I want you to consider doing all of your SITD work free-motion for two reasons:

■ It is very difficult to see what you are doing when using most walking feet. The typical walking foot is pretty long, and it is hard to see "where you're sewing."

■ If the piecing is not perfectly accurate, it is much easier to jog around mismatched intersections with free-motion stitching than it is to stop and raise and lower a walking foot and stop and start the stitching to keep the stitches in-the-ditch. Also, with free-motion stitch in-the-ditch, you don't have to stitch in a straight line from one side of your quilt to the other. By doing your SITD work free-motion with a hopping foot, you can plan a route that will allow you to stitch an irregularly shaped block in-the-ditch in a continuous manner. There may be a little backtracking involved in some cases, but this is still a lot faster than trying to turn the quilt and stitch at angles and so forth.

I prefer to SITD with clear thread, which to me is less obvious when going from one colored piece to another as the ditch moves from side to side. Keep in mind that my quilts get used for trunk shows only. Some people do not like clear thread, and that is just fine.

Pick a thread color that is as unobtrusive as possible and give it a try. If you have some old orphan blocks, and most of us do, sandwich a few and practice SITD on these blocks. I think you will quickly see the advantage of doing this type of work free-motion.

Remember in the 60s when some ladies burned their bras in the name of freedom? Well, here is your chance to get rid of your walking foot in the name of free-motion. Hurrah!

Free-motion stitched in-the-ditch block (includes additional quilting)

Background Designs

At some point in time, you are going to be confronted with a situation where you want your quilted designs to stand out more, or perhaps you might want to make a wholecloth quilt with lots of elegant quilted designs. To accomplish this, the area around the quilted designs must be made to look like background, while at the same time allowing the featured designs to project toward the viewer as much as possible.

What we are trying to do is create a three-dimensional product out of a two-dimensional medium. Hand quilters did this with grids and crosshatching to accentuate the primary quilted designs. To me this is the most beautiful approach, but also the most difficult to do because it is hard to keep the pattern uniformly spaced over the entire quilt top. If you are off just a little with each line, it is easy to get off track.

The most common background quilting design for machine quilters is stippling, but there are many other background design possibilities. Don't be afraid to experiment and come up with your own unique background design.

Many of these designs are very geometric in nature and require only a few simple tools and supplies to lay out. All you really need in the way of tools is a ruler, either a 45°

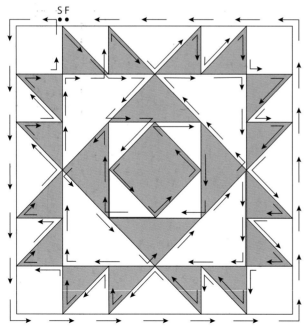
Free-motion stitch in-the-ditch map

or 60° triangle, and a marking device. Masking tape is a handy accessory to have on hand.

CROSSHATCHING

This design typically runs at 45° to the outside edge of the quilt. The diagonal lines can be spaced as close or as far apart as you like. The spacing of the lines can be uniform or at different widths in a set repeating pattern. The most common way of doing this design is to use masking tape as spacers for the lines (see page 54).

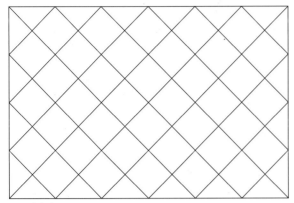
Crosshatching

DIAMONDS

Diamonds are done the same way as crosshatching. The only difference is that a 60° triangle is substituted for the 45° triangle.

If you wanted to create what is called a hanging diamond, you would stitch one set of lines with the 60° triangle, and the other set would be placed parallel to the edge of the quilt.

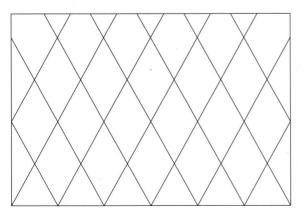
Diamonds

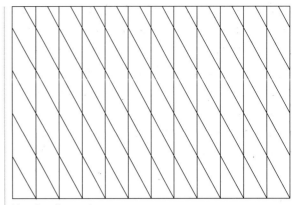
Hanging diamonds

GRID

A grid is done much the same way as the above-mentioned designs, only the lines are parallel and perpendicular to the edges of the quilt.

In all cases extreme care must be taken in laying out these designs, particularly if they go all the way around the quilt. It is very easy for the designs to get skewed as you work your way around the quilt. It is very disheartening to get to the other side of the quilt from where you started and find that the designs do not line up evenly.

Grid

STIPPLING

This background design consists of a series of random, connected arcs and curves. The arcs and curves should all have the same radius, or at least as close as possible. One of the key things that stipplers try not to do is cross over previously stitched lines. I can almost guarantee you that if you do very much stippling, at some point you are going to cross over the stitched line. If the viewers of the quilt have enough time on their hands to look for these little mistakes, I say they should get a life. It is going to happen sometimes, so don't obsess over it.

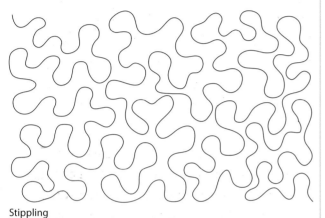
Stippling

1. Sandwich a practice panel of muslin and batting (see page 22).

2. Start stitching and concentrate on making your curves and arcs as smooth as possible. You can make this happen by going as fast as you can while still maintaining control over your motion. The faster you can go, the smoother your curves will be because you do not have time to make any jogs.

At first, your stitching will look very contrived and controlled. The curves are all in a line and are connected by short straight lines.

Beginning stippling; too even and controlled

3. Continue stitching and try to eliminate the short straight lines between the curves and arcs. As soon as you complete an arc or curve, begin making another curve or arc. I liken it to a series of capital S's that are lying on their sides and are linked together one after another. Practice this technique until you can consistently stitch the S's without any straight lines between the curves.

Capital S's connected together

4. The next step is to force yourself to stitch in random directions across the area to be stippled.

When I say "force yourself," that is exactly what I mean. You will probably find it difficult to do this. After all, there is an area right next to where you have stitched that is still unstitched, isn't there? If you do not wander about, your pattern may end up looking contrived rather than random. The wandering can be accomplished by shortening or lengthening the arcs or curves before transitioning into the next one.

Wandering pattern

If you find that you get stuck in your wandering and end up in a corner where you have no way out, do not get upset. All you need to do is end the stitch line and secure the thread ends. Move over to another area next to a previous stitch line and begin again. I do this by starting my next stitch line right on the previous line and then going from there. The new line will create a V shape that looks like a fork in a curved road.

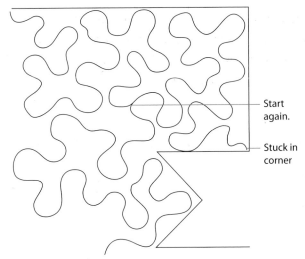

Getting stuck and starting again

Mr. Quilt's Loopy Pattern

Over the years, I have had many of my students say that you can't cross over the lines in stippling. Because of this, I set out to develop a background pattern where it is okay to cross over the lines; in fact, it is mandatory. I am not saying that this is a completely original design, just that it is one that works for me. To me it looks better than stippling because it gives the viewer more visual interest than a flat stippled surface.

The pattern is a series of loops that fill the background surface.

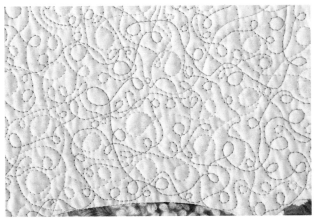

Loopy background

To stitch this design, I usually go over the surface at least 3 times to get the look I want. The first pass consists of a series of loops that are all about the same size. The

only real rule I try to adhere to is that I attempt to avoid stitching through the loops themselves.

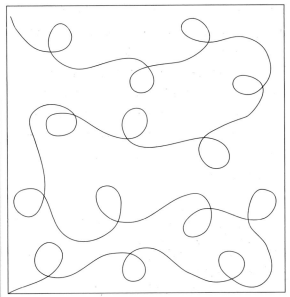

First pass of loops

The second pass of loops is stitched between the stitching of the first pass. Because I have less open space than with the first pass, these loops are going to be a little smaller than the first ones. I will stitch over the other lines with no adverse consequences whatsoever. Once again, the only thing that I try to avoid is stitching through the loops themselves.

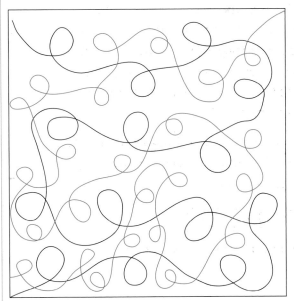

First and second passes

One more pass doing the same thing, and I am finished. This time there is much less open area, so I am forced to make my loops pretty small.

Third and final pass; the illustrations show the 3 passes in different colors for clarity, but usually I stitch it all in the same color or shades of the same color.

When the design is complete, it presents a pebbly textured surface when viewed in indirect light. This creates a lot of visual interest and accomplishes the same thing as stippling and is much easier to do.

Sandwich a practice panel and give it a try. I am sure that within a very short time, you will be doing this like a pro.

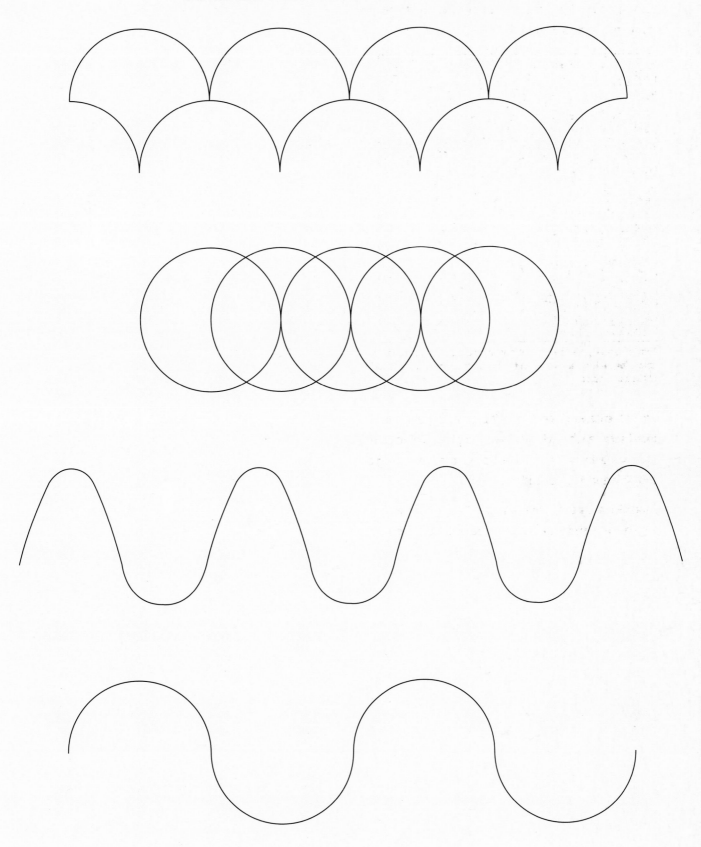

FREE-MOTION MACHINE QUILTING!

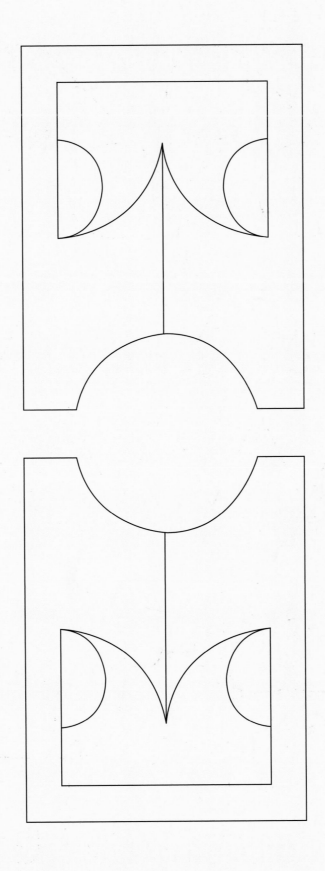

CHAPTER 4

Design Choices and Marking Tips

One of the most perplexing problems facing us is trying to decide what quilting designs we should use to make our quilts look as good as possible. I have always felt that the quilting should enhance the piecer's work. Over the years I have come up with a set of guidelines that have seemed to serve me well.

The first question that you should ask yourself is what is the end use of your quilt. The answer will go a long way in determining how much time should be spent on the quilting.

Notes

■ Chances are you will be doing more quilting than the minimum requirements for your batting, so spacing will not really be an issue for you, but always refer to the batting manufacturer's guidelines on the package to be sure.

■ To make the piecing look as good as possible, stitching in-the-ditch is a must to make each pieced design stand out and to stabilize the quilt. This is not the most exciting part of machine quilting, but it will make a difference in the appearance of your quilt.

■ After stitching in-the-ditch, add simple or more complicated artistic quilting, depending on how much time you want to put into your project. Since I stitch in-the-ditch around all the parts of any pieced block, I do not use a quilting design that covers the entire block itself. I let the piecing be the focal point of the block.

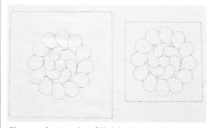

Artistic quilting in open blocks and small open areas in pieced blocks (full quilt, page 65)

Star block stitched in-the-ditch and simple quilting in open areas

■ In the open blocks, fill the block completely with the quilting design. Do not put a 4″ design in an 8″ block. It will look out of place, and the block will appear to be baggy around the outside of the quilted design.

Choose design that fills block completely, as shown on the right.

■ Fresh new designs can be created by taking elements from different designs and combining them to make completely new designs. This is a lot of fun and can be quite liberating. My first book, *Sophisticated Stitches,* has some great designs and examples that show how to do this.

This technique is very useful for those odd-shaped areas that need a quilting design. The components can easily be adjusted to fill the desired area.

◼ Outline stitch around appliquéd elements. This is the same technique as stitch in-the-ditch, only it's around a motif rather than between seams. Once the outlining is done, you can go back and accentuate the individual appliqué elements with colored threads.

Outline appliqué motifs (full quilt, page 61)

What Quilting Designs Are Appropriate for My Quilt?

I can't tell you how many times I have been asked this question, by friends and students alike. They all act like I am an expert on the subject and that what I say is gospel. This couldn't be further from the truth. However, I do have guidelines that help me decide what design to use, but that is all they are—guidelines.

Is the quilt traditional or contemporary? If it is traditional, I know I am pretty safe using designs, or variations of designs, that have been used on antique quilts. Look at pictures of old quilts that have been hand quilted. You will see lots of feathers, ropes, and simple geometric designs that could be drawn with a minimum number of tools. Keep in mind that our quilting ancestors did not have any of the fancy tools and stencils we have access to. They had to make do with what they had around the house. There is no reason we can't do the same when preparing designs that will look every bit as elegant as many of those antique quilts.

If your design has curved piecing or appliqué, consider using angular lines and designs to contrast with the curves and add variety and interest to the overall design. If your quilt's blocks or design is very angular, such as stars, include quilting designs that are more curved and flowing to help soften the angular look of the stars.

Curved and angular quilting designs

If you are working on a contemporary quilt, then to my way of thinking, there are really no rules per se. Rather, I would recommend that you determine what you are trying to say and then work out designs that are going to communicate your message. For example, if the quilt is a landscape with some sky, you might want to quilt the sky so you project the feeling of air movement.

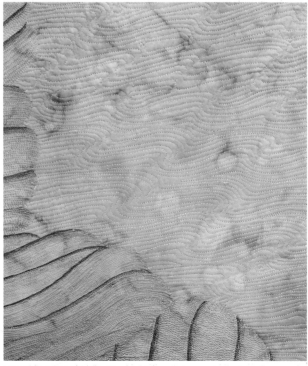

Hot desert wind (full quilt, page 59)

Air movement in night sky (full quilt, page 60)

If there are ribbons or elements that expand or contract, it might be appropriate to quilt curved lines that accentuate the illusion of expansion or contraction.

Expanding and contracting elements (full quilt, page 61)

As you can see, the quilting does not have to be overly elaborate or complicated to be effective. Just look at each different section of the quilt top that needs quilting and ask yourself what you can easily do to make it contribute best to the entire design.

The dirty little secret is that just about anything within reason will make the quilt look great.

Design Transfer and Marking

The most common form of quilting designs are the plastic stencils available at quilt shops or shows. The real problem with stencils is that the designs never seem to fit the area you want to quilt. They are either too large or too small.

You can transfer almost any design from any source to your quilt using the technique that follows. I tend to work from copyright-free books, such as from those from Dover Publishing, so I don't have to worry about copyright issues.

SUPPLIES

- Design—enlarged or reduced to the proper size

- Embroidery hoop large enough to fit around the design

- Fine mesh tulle (light-colored for light fabric and dark-colored for dark fabric)

- Sharpie permanent marking pen (black for light tulle and silver for black tulle)

- Marking device to mark the design on the quilt top.

1. Stretch the tulle tautly in the embroidery hoop.

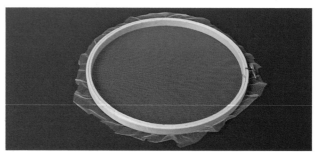

Stretch tulle in hoop.

2. Position the hoop over the design with the tulle against the design lines.

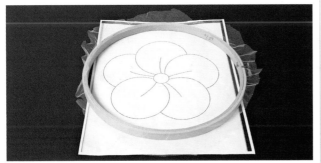

Position hoop over design.

3. Trace the design with the Sharpie marking pen. As a precaution, use a warm iron to set the marked design on the tulle. Take care not to melt the tulle. Then place the marked design on a piece of scrap muslin and trace part of the design with your quilt marking device to test the Sharpie's permanence.

Trace design with marking pen.

Caution: Put the Sharpie pen out of reach before going on to the next step.

4. Place the hoop on the quilt top where you want the design to be located for quilting.

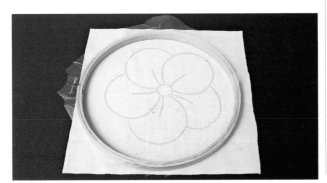

Place hoop in proper location.

5. Trace the design onto the quilt through the tulle with the quilt-marking device.

Trace design onto quilt.

6. Remove the hoop to see the design on your quilt top.

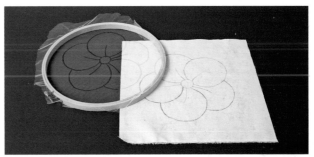

Remove hoop.

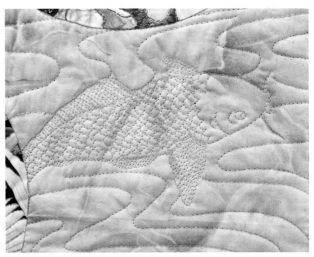

Koi quilted design using tulle technique (full quilt, page 62)

Fabric Print as the Quilting Design

I often use the print of the fabric as my quilting design. The fabric used for the borders will often be a print that you can use as your quilting design by outlining the designs with stitching. If the border fabric is a busy print, a marked and stitched design probably wouldn't show. By using the print of the fabric as your design, you do not have to spend time marking a design, and the viewer will not be distracted by trying to pick out the design in the busyness of the print.

When using this technique, stitch around just a few design elements in the fabric to start with. You can always add more quilting if you need to, but stitching around every element is usually unnecessary.

Stitching around every design element (full quilt, page 58)

Marking Tools

There are many marking tools for sale that purport to make the marking process easier for the quilter. Suffice it to say that some work well, and some are not any good at all. In the words of former President Reagan, "Trust but verify." By that I mean that you must verify that you are going to be able to get your marks out after the quilting is complete. Test the marking device on a scrap of fabric you are going to be quilting on to make sure you can get the marks out. The last thing you want is to have those marks permanently on your quilt.

When I first started machine quilting, there were very few marking tools available, but I was able to come up with some tools that have worked very well for me over the years. I will discuss my favorites and try to give you what I feel are the pros and cons of each. In the end, you will have to decide for yourself what works best for you, depending on the quilt that you are working on at the time.

Stitching around selected designs (full quilt, page 62)

Marking tools

COLLINS WASHABLE FABRIC MARKER

This blue pen has been around for many years and is still one of my favorites. I prefer the one that has a wider line (#C48) rather than the fine-line marker. The fine-line marker makes marks that are just too hard for me to see. These pens work very well on the tulle design technique (see page 50).

You have probably heard many horror stories about these pens, and some of them are probably true, but I think many of the problems you have heard of are not the fault of the pen, but rather operator error. If you use them with care, I think you will be quite happy with these pens.

First of all, you must be willing to soak your quilt in a tub of cold water for about 30 minutes to completely remove all the marks. Just spritzing the marks is not adequate. I have seen the marks go away and then come sneaking back in the form of blue lines or stains. If you don't notice that this has happened and touch them with a hot iron, the marks will turn brown and be there forever, and that is a long time. You should also not expose the marks to bright light or high temperatures for long periods of time.

Another downside to these pens is that they will not show up on darker fabrics.

COLLINS VANISHING FABRIC MARKER

This pen is air erasable; however, water will also erase it. In fact, the pen depends on humidity in the atmosphere to make the marks go away. The package says the marks will last from 12 to 48 hours. That may be true in relatively dry climates, but in areas with high humidity, the marks will only last for a very short time. If you live where it is drier, you might want to give these pens a try, but mark only what you can stitch before the marks disappear. Do not press your work until all of the marks have gone away or those marks will become permanent. I have used these pens for many years with excellent success. They can also be used with the tulle technique (see page 50).

CHALK PENCILS

Chalk pencils are always in my bag of tricks. I make sure that the pencils are pure chalk with no oils or waxes in them. Oil and wax will make it harder to get the marks out. You may or may not have to launder your quilt after the quilting is done. Once again, test before you use it. Oftentimes, the marks can be removed with a clean fingernail brush and/or a damp cloth. The worst-case situation is that you will have to launder your quilt in detergent. Try to get a color of pencil that is barely visible when doing your marking. Do not use a neon color just because it is easier to see. It will be harder to remove later. These pencils will also work well with the tulle technique (see page 50).

The real downside to these pencils is that they get dull very easily, and it is hard to keep a sharp point on them.

POWDERED CHALK

If you are using a traditional plastic stencil, you might want to consider using good old powdered chalk. I get mine from the local hardware store. It is what construction workers use to snap chalk lines. *Use only white.* Do not be tempted by the bright colors. Powdered chalk is also available at quilt shops.

When applying the chalk, I tend to stay away from the pounce pad to cut down on the mess. I put a small amount of chalk in a saucer or shallow box and work from that. By dipping a cotton ball into the chalk and then flicking it with my finger, I find I can eliminate the problem of most of the chalk going everywhere but where I want it to go, thus reducing the mess.

The problem with powdered chalk is getting it to stick to the quilt top long enough to complete your quilting. The chalk needs to be "fixed" to the top. This can be done by lightly spraying the marks with hair spray, spray starch, or spray sizing.

Since you are fixing the chalk to the quilt top, you will have to launder your quilt to remove the chalk and "fixative."

LEAD/GRAPHITE PENCIL

It used to be common for hand quilters to use lead, then graphite, pencils to mark their quilting designs. If you look at some antique quilts carefully, you can still see the pencil marks. Some new pencils on the market supposedly make removable marks. I am a bit leery, but you might want to give them a try. Try them on a scrap of fabric first to make sure you can get the marks out. A hot iron is the enemy.

MASKING TAPE

Masking or painter's tape is excellent to use as a guide for quilting straight lines, grids, or crosshatching. Masking tape tends to stick better than painter's tape, but is harder to see on lighter-colored fabrics. Masking tape should not be left on your quilt for extended periods of time, because it may become very hard to remove.

To stitch a straight line, choose the correct width of tape for your project, lay a ruler down as a guide, and apply the tape next to the ruler. For a grid or crosshatching, use a ruler or triangle to get the proper starting angle and put down several strips of tape next to each other. Peel every other strip away and then stitch on both sides of the tape. As you stitch along the edge of the tape, you will eventually come to a design, a border, or the edge of the quilt. When this happens stitch right on top of the design, in-the-ditch, or outside the border to the next piece of tape. Now all you have to do is go back the other direction.

Tape for grid guide

Be very careful when laying out these straight-line designs; it is very easy to get your alignment off as you progress around the quilt. Make sure you are constantly checking to make sure that everything is properly aligned.

I like to use ½"-wide masking tape as a guide when I am trying to quilt a long, gentle curving line. This is a good way to lay out a curve.

½" tape for curve guide

If you do not like part of the curve, simply lift up the tape and reposition it before doing your stitching. You can probably get a couple of applications out of the tape before it loses its tackiness and has to be thrown away. If you can't find ½"-wide tape anywhere else, an automotive paint store will carry it. This is also true for ¼"-wide masking tape. This tape is good for tight curves, but because it is so narrow, it does not stick as well as the ½".

Echo Quilting

This is a quilting style that is very commonly seen on Hawaiian quilts, but it is a wonderful choice for many other styles of quilts. Parallel lines radiate out around appliquéd or quilted design elements. Some very interesting patterns can evolve as the parallel stitching lines intersect with other parallel lines from different design elements. Echo quilting makes an excellent background pattern to accentuate other quilted designs.

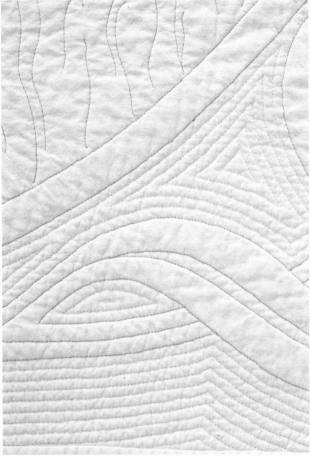

Echo quilting

Echo quilting can be done easily by machine using a hopping foot that has a round base. Use the outside of the foot as a guide that follows the previous line of quilting.

Hopping foot with round base

Making a Design Fit Your Border

Borders are an excellent area to show off your quilting skills, especially if the fabric is one that will show off the stitching.

Border quilting

METHOD 1

The main problem is making the design fit the area you have to work with. I have seen quilts that have a fancy feathered design quilted in the borders, and the design appears to run off the edge with no concern for how it looks.

I want to give you some guidelines for how to make patterns fit in the border and look like they were made just for the area you have to work with.

If you are using a structured pattern, it will have a repeat; this is the place where the preceding pattern starts over again.

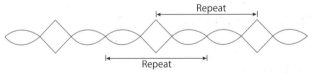

Pattern repeats

We want the pattern repeats to be equally spaced across the border.

1. Mark the corners of the pattern on your quilt. The distance between where the corner patterns end is where we must fit the pattern repeats equally.

Mark corners.

2. Measure the distance between the corner patterns. Let's pretend that this distance is 23″ on one side of our quilt.

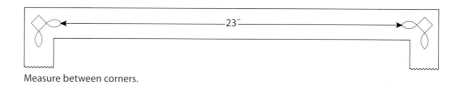

Measure between corners.

3. Measure the length of the pattern repeat. In our example the pattern repeats every 3⅛″.

Measure pattern repeat.

4. With a calculator, divide 3.125″ (size of the repeat) into 23″ (length of the side) (23″ ÷ 3.125″ = 7.36).

The result shows that there are 7 complete repeats with .36 of an eighth repeat left over. If we just merrily went on our way and started marking the border design from left to right without making any adjustments, the repeats would not come out even. There is a pretty large space between the last repeat and the corner, but it is not large enough to add a full repeat.

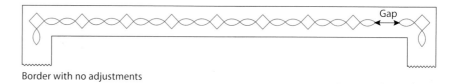

Border with no adjustments

5. To make the adjustment needed, multiply .36 (leftover portion of a repeat) × 3.125″ (length of one repeat) (.36 × 3.125″ = 1.125″). You will get the measurement of the amount we would have leftover after 7 repeats. This means that we must spread 1.125″ equally between the 7 full repeats and the corners.

6. Count the spaces between the corners and the 7 full repeats. There are 8 open spaces.

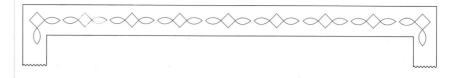

7. Divide 1.125″ (total amount needed) by 8 (the number of spaces between repeats) (1.125″ ÷ 8 = .14″). Each pattern repeat will have to be stretched .14″. The measurement .14″ is somewhere between ⅛″ and ³⁄₁₆″. Now we are beginning to split hairs and get into a lot of math, which most of us do not like.

When we start marking these designs, we are going to fudge a little to make the process as easy as possible. Our goal is to fool the eye into thinking that everything is equally spaced, even though in reality it may not be exact.

8. Put the first repeat on the border so that it is against the left corner of the corner. Stick a pin or make a mark just over ⅛″ (.125″) to the right of the end of the first repeat.

Mark a little over ⅛″ from pattern.

9. As you mark the design, keep scooting the pattern over toward the mark you made in Step 8. The goal is to be at the mark when you finish the first repeat. I find that if there is a curve or loop in the repeat, that is the easiest place to stretch the design.

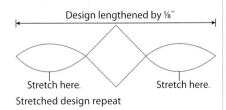

Design lengthened by ⅛″

Stretch here.   Stretch here.

Stretched design repeat

10. Repeat this process for about half of the pattern repeats. Then, go back and start at Step 2 to see if you are on track to come out evenly at the end. It is not critical that every design repeat be stretched the same amount at exactly the same point. Your brain will subconsciously calculate the distances as the same if they are close to being the same.

If our quilt started out 24½″ wide, we would make the same calculation of dividing 3.125″ into 24.5″ (24.5″ ÷ 3.125″ = 7.84″). This means that we would have to stretch the 7 pattern repeats and absorb 3.125″ × .84, or 2.65″, between the repeats. In this case it would be far easier to add an eighth pattern and shrink all 8 repeats. We would only have to shrink .48″ rather than stretching 7 repeats by 2.65″.

METHOD 2

If you have a border design that has a very long repeat, it can be difficult to stretch or shrink the pattern enough without causing distortion to the design. If you are confronted with this problem, there are a couple of easy solutions that work every time. In fact, they will also work for border designs with a shorter repeat.

1. Find the exact center of the border length and draw a line across the width.

2. Draw the pattern from the corner to the centerline of the border.

3. Flip the pattern over and repeat the process from the right corner to the center.

Pattern running into itself at centerline

METHOD 3

The other solution is to find a block quilting design the same width as your border design and mark it on the centerline.

Repeat Steps 2 and 3 above and allow the repeating border components to run into the design in the center.

Pattern running into center design

I encourage you not to be afraid to experiment with designs. I think you will be pleasantly surprised at how good they will look on your quilts.

Asian Salsa, 52″ × 64″.
Pieced and quilted by the author.

Equally spaced curved quilting lines accentuate the feeling of movement. The print of the fabric was used as the quilting designs for the rest of the quilt. The black background was very densely quilted with a very small looping pattern.

Noshi, 66″ × 74″.
Pieced and quilted by the author.

Curved elements have curved quilting lines to give the feeling of the pieces contracting. The background was quilted with a looping design. Three shades of the same color of thread were used to create visual interest. A larger looping pattern was used as the quilting design in the border.

Swahili Maiden, 41″ × 31″.
Painted and quilted by the author.

A piece of batik fabric was used as the basis for this quilt. The image was first painted with transparent acrylic paint and then quilted using complementary threads to accentuate the stitching. The background was quilted in a swirling design to create the illusion of hot desert air currents blowing around the lady.

Stormy Seas, 60″ × 60″.
Pieced, appliquéd, and quilted by the author.

Curved quilting lines accentuate the waves, the curved fullness of the sails, and the cliffs. The print of the fabric was used as the design for the quilting on the cranes and the border. The stars in the night sky were quilted with metallic thread.

Split Decision, 41″ × 54″.
Pieced and quilted by the author.

This quilt was inspired by an art deco textile design. Curved elements have curved quilting lines to give the feeling of the pieces contracting. The background is a variation of a clamshell pattern. The print of the primary printed fabric elements was used as the quilting design. Simple geometric designs were used in the rest of the quilted areas.

Pacific Flyway, 46″ × 56″.
Pieced and quilted by the author.

Curved elements have curved quilting lines to give the feeling of the pieces contracting. The background was quilted with curving lines to simulate the feeling of water. In addition to the curving lines, koi fish were quilted in the background. The print of the circle motifs was also used as the quilting pattern to accentuate the design of the fabric. The print of the border fabric was used as the quilting design in the border. Various elements were outlined with gold metallic thread.

Out of Africa, 48″ × 58″.
Pieced and quilted by the author.

Curved elements have curved quilting lines to give the feeling of the pieces contracting. The print of the background was used as the quilting design. Additional ghost quilting was added to match the print quilting. The print of the circle motifs was also used as a quilting pattern to accentuate the design of the fabric. A structured quilting design was used in the border, but it is hard to see because of the print of the fabric.

Lady Liberty Walking, 53″ × 64″.
Quilted by the author.

The inspiration for this quilt came from an old half-dollar that was designed by Augustus Saint Gaudens. This quilt was finished in 2001 and is my 9/11 tribute quilt to the wonderful country that I live in. Gold metallic thread was used on the image, and a natural-colored thread was used for the echo quilting.

Improved Nine-Patch, 48″ × 61″.
Pieced and quilted by the author.

This is a pattern that dates back to the 1930s. All colored pieces were stitched in-the-ditch. Simple geometric quilting was used on the small square white pieces to offset the more complicated traditional designs in the rest of the white pieces. A very traditional feather was used to quilt the border.

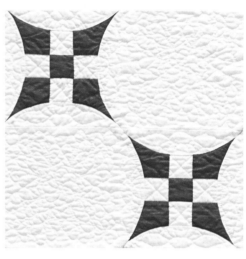

Lady in Red, 41″ × 58″.
Painted and quilted by the author.

A piece of batik fabric was used as the foundation of this quilt. The images were painted on the fabric with transparent acrylic paints. Complementary threads were then used to stitch over the painted elements. Victorian designs were quilted into the background, and then a looping pattern was used to highlight the Victorian designs.

Auntie's Clam Chowder, 53˝ × 66˝.
Pieced and quilted by the author.

This quilt is made from pieced clamshell components. All colored pieces were stitched in-the-ditch. The background quilting is similar to what would be seen on a wholecloth quilt. Traditional designs were used with thread that matches the fabric.

Grandma's Flower Pot, 49″ × 59″.
Assembled and quilted by the author.

These blocks are original blocks from the 1930s. The muslin squares were called penny blocks and were sold at mercantile stores. Women would then appliqué feed-sack material onto the premarked patterns. Appliquéd pieces were outlined with stitching, and then traditional designs were used in the background and the sashing.

Sophisticated Stitches, 46″ × 55″.
Quilted by the author.

This is a wholecloth quilt that uses some of the designs from my book *Sophisticated Stitches*. The design elements are machine trapuntoed to get greater definition. The background features a very dense stippling to further increase the definition of the designs.

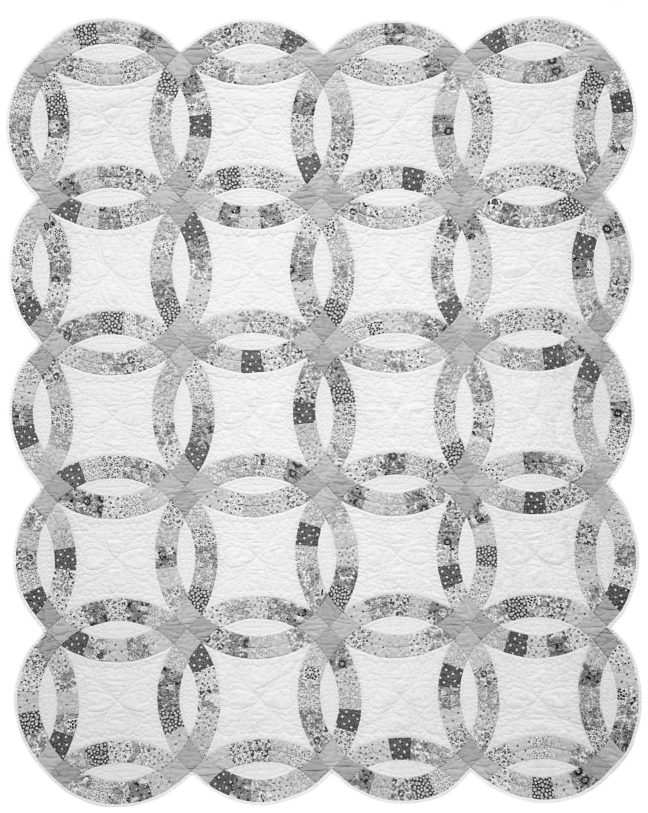

Don & Donna's Double Wedding Ring, 56″ × 69″.
Pieced and quilted by the author.

Traditional quilting designs were used in the open areas with thread that matches the fabric. This is a very traditional-looking quilt.

Xuberance, 48″ × 63″.
Pieced and quilted by the author.

Curved lines were used to give the feeling of movement in the curved pieces. The design motifs in the large floral print were used as the quilting design.

note:

All designs on pages 71–76 are 3". Enlarge as needed to fit your quilt blocks.

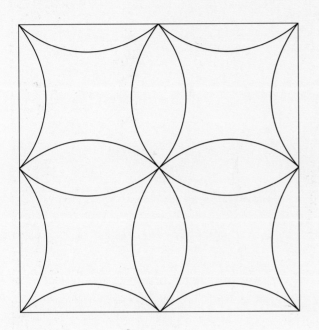

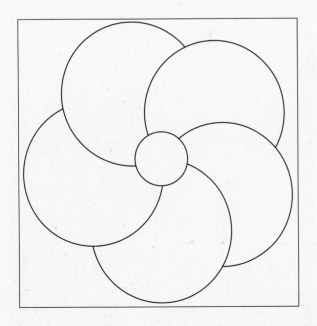

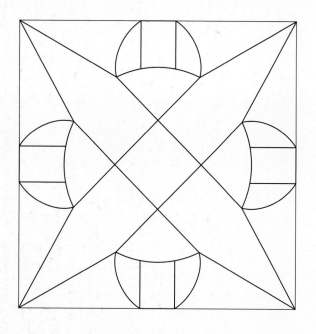

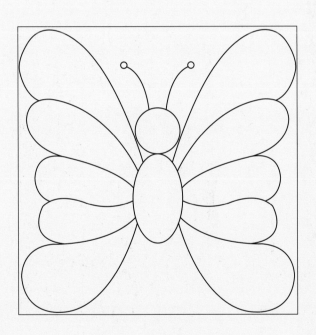

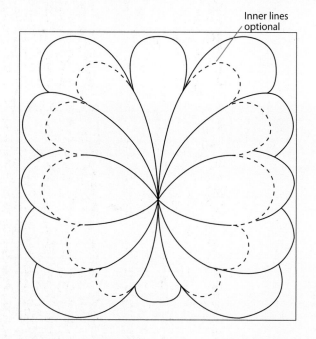

Inner lines
optional

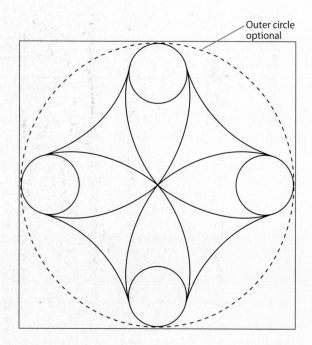

Outer circle
optional

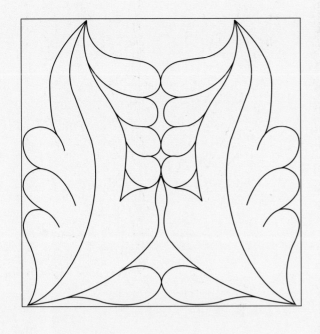

ABOUT THE AUTHOR

Don started his adventure in quilting as a longarm quilter for others. Many of his customers expressed interest in learning to do the style of quilting that he did. As a result of those requests, he transferred the skills he had developed in his quilting business to home machines. The only real difference is that with a home machine, you are moving the quilt sandwich, while the machine is doing this with a longarm machine. The stitching techniques are exactly the same.

He says that probably his greatest reward is seeing students walk into a class saying that there is no way they will be able to stitch complicated heirloom feathers in one day, and being able to prove them wrong time and time again.

Also by Don Linn

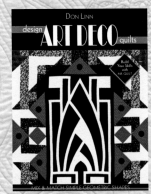

Also available as an eBook

Also available as an eBook

Great Titles *from* C&T PUBLISHING & STASH BOOKS

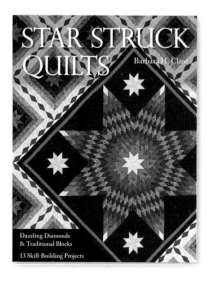

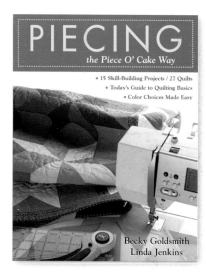

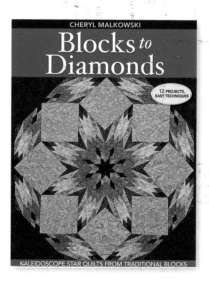

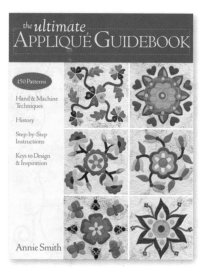

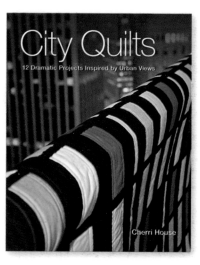

Available at your local retailer or **www.ctpub.com** *or* **800-284-1114**

For a list of other fine books from C&T Publishing, visit our website to view our catalog online.

C&T PUBLISHING, INC.

P.O. Box 1456
Lafayette, CA 94549
800-284-1114

Email: ctinfo@ctpub.com
Website: www.ctpub.com

C&T Publishing's professional photography services are now available to the public. Visit us at www.ctmediaservices.com.

Tips and Techniques can be found at www.ctpub.com > Consumer Resources > Quiltmaking Basics: Tips & Techniques for Quiltmaking & More

For quilting supplies:

COTTON PATCH

1025 Brown Ave.
Lafayette, CA 94549
Store: 925-284-1177
Mail order: 925-283-7883

Email: CottonPa@aol.com
Website: www.quiltusa.com

Note: Fabrics used in the quilts shown may not be currently available, as fabric manufacturers keep most fabrics in print for only a short time.